Emotional Intelligence for Leadership

Coleman Christy Tanos

Published by Coleman Christy, 2023.

EMOTIONAL INTELLIGENCE FOR LEADERSHIP

First edition. December 25, 2023.

ISBN: 979-8223297826

Written by Coleman Christy Tanos.

Table of Contents

EMOTIONAL INTELLIGENCE FOR LEADERSHIP

****

Improve the skills of emotional intelligence (EQ): self-awareness, self-discipline, motivation, empathy, social skills, assertiveness and resilient.
By: Coleman Christy Tano

____

INTRODUCTION

Why is it important for us to understand emotional intelligence? Are there different types of parts? Is there a difference between people who do different types of work?

Emotional intelligence can be learned and developed. Now there are many ways to teach and learn emotional intelligence. With the right decision and commitment, you can improve your current level. Not as cognitive as in old age is emotional intelligence (IQ), which reaches its peak at the age of seventeen and remains constant throughout life until its decreasing intelligence can be improved at any age. As your emotional experience increases by using emotional inventory (EQ), you can ensure that emotional intelligence increases with age and peaks in the age group of forty to forty-nine and then decreases. This can mean that after forty-nine years, few new experiences increase or improve our emotional intelligence. However, learning about ourselves is a lifelong task. Emotional intelligence improves with age and increases between youth and early youth. The needs of each individual are different. We all live together with other people, in our family, in our community, in our environment or in our profession, and we are able to understand, understand and take the opportunity to decide if it is good for all of us.

However, different functions may require different levels and aspects of emotional intelligence. For example, if you work in a job with a high level of contact with other people, you may need to be able to manage your emotions better (to manage storms) and since you are a consultant you may need to be able to manage them better. To understand problems. There are differences between men and women. Women are aware of their feelings, show more compassion, communicate better with their personality and behave more socially than men. On the other hand, men seem to have better self-esteem and more respect, more autonomy, better stress management, more flexibility, better problem solving and more optimism than women.

"Emotional intelligence contributes to your general intelligence. Whether you are systematic, grocery shopping in a supermarket or entrepreneurs to plan and reach an action plan or even your life goals, you need good intelligence as a quotient "Focusing on emotional intelligence does not mean getting rid of the patterns and structures you learned long ago to organize your daily life. A conscience for the emotional aspects of what happens will increase the capacity of people with an IQ. Identically distinguish is their actual ability to deal with the environment. Emotional intelligence "is not so alaximoron

Eximoron is a phrase or word that combines two contradictory ideas (such as "bittersweet", "living death"). In an apparent contradiction, "emotional intelligence" is the depth of the concept. Emotional intelligence: includes both the process of becoming emotions, which are sometimes considered "soft" things, and the need to analyze emotions and learn new skills in a "difficult" analysis. The term "emotional intelligence" has highlighted this important combination of thought and feeling. Both are necessary to make good decisions. The hard sciences that support it Neuroscience, medicine and psychology have contributed to our understanding of emotions and the role of emotions in maintaining health. This affects our ability to make decisions. We make the most of our choices through our decisions, believe it or not. Therefore, it is useful to make good decisions.

Why is emotional intelligence important? EQ may not be as well known as IQ, but many experts consider it more important than IQ. Why? Studies show that EQ is a better indicator of success, the quality of relationships and a person's happiness. It is visible everywhere and critical in all areas of life. Have you heard someone say, "Wow, what a positive person? You get something exceptional in life!" or "Such a person is very loving and sociable, a great leader". These comments show that a person who has a high EQ, even if he doesn't know he is seen and heard by others. It is these types of individuals that others believe can be successful

Why is EQ important for everyone? EQ is an absolutely vital part of forming, developing, maintaining and improving personal relationships with others. There is no denying that people who know how to build positive relationships with other people are likely to succeed in their field. High equalization workers can work harmoniously in teams and adapt to change. No matter how smart you are, if you have little emotional intelligence, you can find the way to success a fight. However, there is good news. Rest assured that you can improve your equalization skills at any age and regardless of your previous behaviors.

EMOTIONAL INTELLIGENCE

Having a deep thought on relationships - you usually closely observe people with emotional intelligence: they maintain close relationships and feel comfortable with themselves and with others. Measurable there have been numerous studies that show that focusing on emotional intelligence has a positive impact on health, business performance and relationships. The benefits include lower blood pressure, increased personal productivity and team effectiveness, and these benefits are maintained six months after learning the techniques. The mindset approach is based on understanding how people, including CEOs, act, confront and behave. The combination of this approach with a comprehensive business experience and the practice of developing the individual's emotional intelligence differs from other development consulting companies in each job. You have almost certainly heard of the emotional quotient, EQ and emotional intelligence, but have you ever wondered if you are emotionally intelligent? Are you emotionally intelligent at work? What is a leader? If you have been thinking about these questions, you may have wondered why emotional intelligence is so important. In this book, we will discuss more about emotional intelligence and its importance for every person, every job, every society and even the world. What is emotional intelligence?

Emotional intelligence is "the ability to perceive emotions, to access and create emotions, to understand emotions and emotional knowledge and to regulate emotions reflexively in order to promote emotional and intellectual growth". In simple terms, it is the measure in which we recognize, or understand, manage, adapt and control our emotions, which motivates us. Take the right actions to reach a goal and achieve empathy for other people and have strong social skills and ability to build positive relationships with others. Emotional intelligence is measured by standardized tests and the result of these tests is called emotional quotient (EQ). The higher your EQ, the better. Unlike the intelligence quotient (IQ), which is often set to a certain age, most scientists and psychologists believe that EQ is malleable and can be improved and learned.

Being aware of yourself means dealing with constructive criticism. If you would probably agree that there is no perfect person in the world and that in everything we do, we need criticism and other people's communication to improve us. If you have a high EQ, you are aware of yourself. This means understanding your strengths, acknowledging your weaknesses, and understanding how your actions affect other people in your environment. The high EQ allows you to use these ratings as an opportunity to improve your performance. This is an essential part of working in an environment with many stakeholders. Self-motivated people can inspire everyone. When a person is motivated, other people in their environment often rate their own motivation. A motivated person is optimistic and motivated by what really matters. Who does not want a motivated person, right? The motivation is contagious and a highly motivated home, a highly motivated workplace or a highly motivated society always surpass the unmotivated. Low motivation can be a sign that your emotional quotient in one or more of the key quadrants of the equalizer is low. EQ makes the world real. People with a high emotional quotient have compassion that allows them to connect with others on an "emotional level". If a person is able to empathize with others, then they will work sincerely and look after the needs of others with compassion and care even in challenging times. A high EQ means that you can master yourself in all situations. All your colleague furiously yells at you for some unknown reason. In that scenario, would that be able to control your emotions and not act the way they do. EQ depends on how we control our positive and negative emotions. Think about some decisions in your life that you are not proud of. Have a deep thought on the cause of lack of self-control or lack of impulse control. The answer can be surprising. Do you have more clarity about what emotional intelligence and emotional quotient are? Do you agree that being "smart in books" or having a high IQ is more important? Can you understand why EQ is the key to success? Take emotional intelligence as the missing link. You know when you see it, even if you can't identify it.

The challenge is that the lack of emotional intelligence is not always easy to spot. It is often clear that there is a problem, but it is a mystery what the problem is. Ask yourself the following question: are you an emotionally intelligent person at home and at work? If the response is yes, you are on the right track! Continue on this path and strengthen your balance on the road to success. If your answer is no, don't worry. Emotional intelligence is a mass of skills that can be carefully improved and a solid strategy. No matter where you are today, you cannot go wrong by investing in yourself and improving your emotional intelligence skills. Is improving your emotional intelligence on your priority list? Why is it important for us to understand emotional intelligence? What are the types of emotional intelligence? What are the differences between men, women and also people of different age performing different types of jobs? Emotional intelligence can be learned and developed. Now there are different ways to teach and learn about emotional intelligence. With the right support, activities, and commitment, you can improve your current level. Increase your vital experience. Emotional intelligence increases with age, peaking in the age group of forty to forty-nine and then subsiding. This could mean that few new experiences will expand or enhance our emotional intelligence. However, learning about ourselves is a lifelong task between youth and early adulthood.

The needs of each person are different. We all live among other people, in our family, community, place or profession, and it is useful for all of us to understand, interpret and use the emotional content of life. However, different activities may require different levels and aspects of emotional intelligence. For example, if you work in a job that involves strong contact with other people, you may need more skills to deal with emotions or to deal with storms while as a counselor you may need more ability to understand your own feelings. There are series of differences between men and women.

On the other hand, men seem to have better self-esteem, to be more independent, to be better at dealing with stress, to be more flexible, to solve problems better and to be more optimistic than women. In order to be able to systematically shop for groceries in a supermarket or to organize that a business plan is created and achieved, or even to achieve your life goals, you need a good IQ (Intellectual Coefficient). To achieve this, some are practical Knowledge required: Focusing on emotional intelligence does not mean discarding the patterns and structures you learned long ago to organize your daily life. IQs can make a difference for people with identical IQs because they can be more effective with the environment.

Emotional intelligence is not a contradiction. An oxymoron is a word or phrase that combines two contradictory ideas (for example "bittersweet", "living death"). What seems to be a contradiction is "emotional intelligence", the depth of the concept of EI: it involves both the process of becoming emotional things, sometimes "soft", and the need to analyze emotions and new skills in a "difficult" way " Analysis to communicate. His hard work in neurology, medicine and psychology has contributed to our understanding of emotions and the role of emotions in maintaining good health. This affects our decision-making capacity. We take most decisions through our emotions, believe it or not. Therefore, it is useful to make good decisions. Reflected in Relationships this is the area in which you normally observe people with emotional intelligence they maintain close relationships and feel comfortable with themselves and with others. Stress has always been gone and will probably always go hand in hand with work. Unfortunately, the stress seems to increase. People with high emotional intelligence report a better mood, fewer fears and fewer worries in times of tension and stress than those with less ability to identify and manage their emotions. Emotional intelligence, however, is not just about naive optimism or obscuring negative emotions by forcing you to make a happy face. Emotionally intelligent people feel less stress. The emotionally intelligent people have upgrade their enabling to incorporate their emotions and their rational thinking at the same time. This leads to a more restrained and comfortable response to stressful circumstances. As you gain EQ, you feel less stressed. Without consciously trying to control our stress responses, people with a high EQ show fewer physical signs of stress reactions, such as: As sweaty hands, high heart rate and increased secretion of certain brain hormones and chemicals. In a situation where most people climb the walls, a person with a high EQ approaches the stressor with the same serenity that most people show only in the most trivial circumstances. In other words, emotionally intelligent people not only claim to experience less stress, but also less physical and mental stress.

REASONS FOR EMOTIONAL INTELLIGENCE

Why Emotional Intelligence Is Important is that emotionally intelligent people value their environment differently. They call pleasant thoughts or memories to counteract their current emotional state, thinking about what steps they need to take to get the problem under control and put it into perspective. On the contrary, they seem less likely to blame themselves for the occurrence of the problem and / or for their inability to solve it. "Second and perhaps most importantly, people who are good with emotions are more likely to choose a coping strategy that focuses on the problem." Every problem we encounter has two options: you can tackle the problem directly or head in the sand, waiting for the problem to resolve itself. People who use a coping strategy that focuses on the problem pay attention to solving the problem instead of ignoring it. Designing a plan will make you feel more relaxed and controlled.

People love challenging jobs, crossword puzzles because solving problems is mentally stimulating. In contrast, less emotionally intelligent people turn their anxiety and fear into a coping strategy that "avoids problems" and only lengthens the tension. As you can imagine, these two strategies become a self-fulfilling prophecy that confirms the conviction that the problem is too difficult to handle. The habit of avoiding problems does not make you forget them. Instead, you wallow in the negative emotions that come with a serious challenge. The problem itself remains a constant source of stress and aggravates the bad feelings that make it difficult to deal with stress. Theoretically, you could take a short cut by omitting emotional intelligence and simply learning adaptive coping skills. The only problem is that people who do not handle emotions well can also misuse a problem-oriented strategy. Only the emotionally intelligent group, which knows how to ward off distractions through fear, grief, anger, jealousy, shame, and the like, can effectively implement a problem-centered approach.

EQ Training the gift that is always passed on. Fortunately, virtually anyone can develop emotional intelligence through training. How to Overcome Your Stress is that you can begin to reduce your stress by improving your own emotional intelligence. A little training in emotional intelligence is very helpful in relieving stress and overcoming the obstacles that inevitable life brings along your path. Emotional intelligence includes a set of skills that help us to perceive, understand, and influence our own and others' emotions. Jobs that do not have these skills or that do not encourage people to use them are not fun jobs. In addition, they are unlikely to be as effective or productive in the long run as the company's employees never connect and really work together. For long-term success, companies need leaders who inspire people and connect the hearts and minds of all employees. These companies need emotionally intelligent executives. Leaders with a high level of emotional intelligence are associated with the people around them. They present themselves as authentic and empathetic, ready to practice expansive thinking and to constantly try to include and understand rather than exclude and ignore. This means a strong and empowering leadership that does not fear the opinions of others and does not feel the need to make the final decision or always prove to be right. These leaders are focused and in control of themselves and the world around them. This creates trust and creates an atmosphere in which employees work together to achieve the best possible results for the company.

The question is: who do we think about when we think about our personal experiences with emotionally intelligent leadership? The sad truth is that, at least for most of us in the places where we work, there is a relative lack of these people. Most companies still believe that emotions and feelings have no value and reward people, not how they get results, but WHAT results they deliver. When we look at our own experiences, we are much more likely to remember distracted and busy executives who have no time to listen or really do not listen, even when they sit in front of us and look at our mouths moving. The good news is that emotionally intelligent leaders are out there somewhere and some companies are even actively trying to encourage these people. These companies open up no path for innovation and state-of-the-art practice. They simply accept that there is a better way to do things. They believe that it is possible to create a better job, and that assessing and developing the skills required is far from being a space science: in fact, it is a proven practice that has been around for years. These companies try to identify and develop the five practices that all emotionally intelligent leaders have in common. They perceive their own feelings and understand them. Effectively express how they feel. Adjust the feelings and emotions of others. Handling facts and feelings for great results. Positively influence your own feelings and those of others. Emotionally intelligent leaders perceive and understand their own emotions: Emotionally intelligent leaders understand how events and triggers in the workplace lead to emotional reactions. They understand that these emotional responses are based on prejudices created by the combination of their experiences, beliefs and values. They are aware of how this cocktail of perceptions and the loose memory of facts influence them, what behaviors can arise (if that influence is not controlled), and what those behaviors and emotions can mean for the people they work with. The result of this knowledge is that they are aware of the effects that their feelings and emotions have on their thinking processes, thereby minimizing the times when this can affect their effectiveness at work. This strengthens your decision making immeasurably. Being aware of their personal emotions and their manifestation, they also connect more with their employees.

Emotionally intelligent leaders understand which events trigger strong emotions and are aware of when that happens. This allows them to adequately express these feelings, to better manage the situation in a constructive way and, above all, to avoid the negative impact on the employee who caused the problem in the first place. Emotionally intelligent leaders effectively express how they feel: by understanding their own emotions, emotionally intelligent executives become better able to express themselves. This ability enables them to help others understand and participate in decisions while being more authentic with the people they work with. This understanding and authenticity enhances your interpersonal relationships across the enterprise, greatly enhancing your interpersonal effectiveness. This enhanced emotional expression creates trust and mutual understanding with your peers, where better collaboration and cooperation arise. Instead of being perceived as "vulnerable" by expressing themselves, these leaders gain hearts and minds with a fair amount of honesty. The key is that they learn to express themselves in the right way, to the right extent and with the right people at the right time and with the right people. There are two benefits to a leader's company that can be adequately expressed. First, there are no surprises, and people know how they relate to these people. This drastically reduces "elusive" behaviors and promotes open dialogue. Secondly, their honesty allows everyone in the business to better understand and interpret the choices they make. This will involve employees more in these decisions and increase the likelihood that their execution will be complete and appropriated.

Emotionally intelligent executives "tune in" with the emotions and feelings of others. Emotionally intelligent executives know that this is absolutely true, and "tune in" with the feelings and emotions of their employees and feel they are trying to understand what it drives and stimulates. These leaders spend time learning how their employees think and feel, and above all, spending time demonstrating and constructively using that knowledge. These behaviors create strong interpersonal relationships between employees and leaders. These are the bonds that form the basis for a highly committed and motivated workforce. The strong emotional attachment of an employee to an executive always exceeds commitment to the organization as a whole, and the motivation that emanates from a passionate and inspirational leader is always beyond the motivation that brings with it a reward or the threat of punishment. People forget what you said, people will forget what you did, but people will never forget how you make them feel about you and themselves and how you made them feel about others). Emotional Smart Leaders can make better decisions by being more expansive and inclusive. This will allow them to build more effective teams, play with people's strengths and understand limitations and "blind spots" at the same time. Each employee in turn leads to a more energetic collaboration that "does things" and promotes more innovation. These leaders view emotions and emotions as vital that should not be overlooked and is generally based on important subconscious thoughts, experiences and knowledge. Through the feelings and emotional aspect of each employee, you can help people stay open, explore and replicate ideas as they ride the bus and expose employees to situations that make the most of them. Have you ever wondered why there is not much collaboration or cooperation in some companies? The answer is probably the way executives and employees who reflect their behavior deal with facts and feelings. The facts are treated with a premium: the currency with which knowledge and status are acquired.

Emotions, however, hamper decisions based on facts. They create no added value and cloud the water. The challenge with this approach is that everyone has feelings. Dealing with facts, not feelings, has only one unavoidable conclusion: a business where people do not care or understand each other. It is therefore not surprising that the people who work in these companies do not work together or cooperate. They are too busy with facts to worry about the people sitting next to them. Emotionally intelligent leaders have a positive influence on their own feelings and those of others. Being aware of oneself and others' feelings and then expressing and arguing with those feelings is only the beginning. Once emotionally intelligent leaders are aware of how they and others are feeling and what the consequences of those feelings are, they want to actively manage and control them in a way that leads to dramatically improved outcomes for the business. This active management and active control makes them resilient and not emotional and does not strengthen their employees indifferently. Their observable behavior makes them seem more focused and controlled and calming their environment. These emotions and behaviors are contagious with the positivity that generates positivity. They develop this control and proactive management through reactive emotional management techniques such as breath control and proactive emotional management techniques such as changing their mentality from negative to positive in relation to certain situations.

A reputation based on precision and accuracy in his work that creates trust and encourages customers to call orders faster than they could be processed. The problem was that the company needed new systems. The old ones were outdated, inefficient and had to be replaced. But how does that work with customers over the next six months? The only solution was the implementation in the execution. The new system would always have a first customer. It was just a risk that needed to be managed. However, the complexity and severity of the problem soon increased. Not by bad planning, but by a collision of unforeseen events came at the worst time to a collapse in the implementation of the new system. Ultimately, emotionally intelligent leaders have a profound impact on our lives. They help to center and connect the world around, to approach us and to feel part of something special. They create trusting and collaborative workplaces that encourage people to think, gather ideas, and guide them through the business to find places to grow and thrive. They motivate and involve each and every one of us, including ourselves, and use the internal sources of power and drive that give us meaning in our lives and make us feel like we belong to them. It's not about strategy, it's about execution.

Therefore, the problem for each of us is that it is enough to do something about it.

"Before you become a leader, success is about developing yourself - if you are a leader, success is about making others grow." Sales managers and contractors who work hard spend hours training and training their sales teams. In too many scenarios your efforts fail. The sales team is not constantly executing its new sales and prospecting capabilities. The excuses vary from "I forgot" to "I feel unwell" or "I'm preparing". The motivated sales manager listens and invests even more time and energy in the placement of sales skills and techniques. Stop the madness! The reason your sales team is not running may have nothing to do with sales skills. It's all about lack of soft skills, also known as emotional intelligence skills. At that moment, you might think, what the hell is emotional intelligence? Why should sales organizations worry? Is it the latest fashion? Can soft skills really lead to hard sales results? Emotional intelligence perceive emotions, understand why emotions are felt, and adapt actions to achieve better results. This is the business model for the "return of emotions". People with high emotional intelligence earn more money. What was the cause of the different results? The same trainer provided the same sales content with different results. Disturbing this behavior, it led us to explore emotional intelligence to determine the missing link among sales training and sales results. Emotional intelligence training assist sales managers better diagnose enactment issues and make their role more effective Leaders and Sales Managers Sales executives with this knowledge base develop sales teams that consistently achieve sales goals even in difficult economic times. Selling ™ is a unique sales approach that combines an advisory sales process with capabilities of Emotional Intelligence Identifies gaps where training is required for soft skills rather than or parallel to training in sales skills. Emotional self-confidence: First things first: A successful sales manager has several titles: teacher, doctor, consultant and coach. The common denominator in all titles is the responsibility to help people to improve. The first step in helping people improve is the proper identification and diagnosis of problems and challenges. As a professional sales manager, the first diagnostic area is to examine the confidence of your salesperson: the foundation of emotional intelligence.

Emotional self-esteem is the ability to recognize personal feelings, to know why you experience emotions, and to lead feelings to a better result. In simple words: "Know thyself." Many well-intentioned sales managers spend hours training sales techniques just to help sellers come up with solutions early, make arrangements, or fail to meet all buying influences. These bad sales behaviors are not resolved by more training in sales techniques. Instead, work with your sales team to deal with the emotions caused by difficult prospects and lead to bad sales. When a salesman allows emotions to go crazy, the brain freezes. Sales reactions that were practiced during the role play are not saved. The seller loses control of the call and becomes an expensive answering machine. "What's your price, who else do business with, why choose your business?" The result is a price-driven sale; it is not a value-oriented sale. It is useful to comprehend how the brain works to understand the emotions and resulting actions of a salesperson. There is a part of the brain that receives all the incoming stimuli, the amygdala. It is a mass of gray almond-shaped matter found in the temporal lobe of the brain known as the "reptilian brain" or "old brain." The task of the almond is to absorb and evaluate all the stimuli that reach the brain. It's like a porter at the front desk. Just as a salesman must receive the porter's sympathy to reach the decision maker, a salesperson must also be aware of the similarity of the almond in order to influence the buying decisions. This knowledge about the brain is also important if you inform your sales team about the reactions during a sales pitch. Can they deal with their emotions in a more difficult perspective and think rationally, or do they enter a combat or flight mode? "The emotionally intelligent salesman controls their emotions to provide an answer that redirects the sales call to a qualified conversation Studies which show that every successful people manage their emotions excellently. Take the place of a litigator as a prosecutor. Is the competent law obtaining the process or ability of the lawyer to manage the many dynamics that occur in the classroom? D. H. A severe judge or an opposing lawyer who says "object" every 60 seconds? The answer is both: a good lawyer needs knowledge of the law and skills to deal with a tough opponent Let's look at the sales professional now Is it the experience that wins agreements or the ability to handle the dynamics. Your sales team to become aware of its problems. Slowing down and analysis of sales talks Analyze the emotions and unproductive actions that occur in a difficult time and discover the cause of the emotions. The number one attribute, which makes very successful people to improve their self-esteem, is slower. It is during idle time that people can be introspective and reflect on their actions during the day. "You must force yourself to stay away from the hustle and bustle up your work to return to reality."

Thanks to downtime, you can ask thoughtful questions and think about them: what was the reason for my reaction? What would have been a better answer? When a person has time to think, the result is more clarity, creativity and positive change. The emotionally intelligent salesman knows that stimuli cannot always be changed (prospects and difficult customers), but one thing can be controlled ... the reaction. Emotional intelligence, also known as EI, is a person's innate ability to perceive, assess and influence the emotions and emotions of others in their environment. The term emotional intelligence itself has emerged from emotional intelligence, which defined it as the ability to understand and reason with feelings. We divide emotional intelligence down into four Parts: Self-knowledge: The ability and the need to understand one's own emotions, to know what those emotions are, and to acknowledge these feelings. Need Management: This is the ability to process emotions in a way relevant to the current situation.

Self-motivation: The ability to stay focused on one goal despite your self-doubt and impulsiveness. Empathy: The ability to engage with the feelings of others and to effectively understand them as they understand themselves. Relationship Management: Ability to handle conflict negotiation and mediation by third parties. What is the reason for the importance of emotional intelligence? Although the volume of quantitative empirical cognitive research is missing in emotional intelligence, research in the field of cognitive learning has shown that emotional intelligence is an essential fundamental aspect of learning. Self-confidence, self-control, curiosity, communication skills, willingness to cooperate, enthusiasm and intentionality. All these features are aspects of emotional intelligence. More recently, social scientists have begun to expose the similarities of emotional intelligence to other psychological bodies, such as: leadership, group performance, individual performance, interpersonal exchange, achievement evaluation and change management.

HOW TO IMPROVE YOUR LEVEL OF EMOTIONAL INTELLIGENCE

Human is a social being, and our success in dealing with people is closely related to our emotional intelligence. Improving the Level of Emotional Intelligence Researchers and scientists see the intelligence quotient, also referred to as I.Q. is fixed, meaning that it does not change throughout life. This is very different from I.Q. In this E.I It can be improved through a combination of life experience, maturity, mindset and stamina. You can improve your emotional intelligence by doing the following: Thinking of the last moment you can think when you've hurt someone's feelings, analyze what your reactions were at that point, and analyze them what you have done to the other person's emotional pain. Try to put yourself in the other's place and empathize with him and his feelings by saying those words. In this exercise, you will effectively improve your understanding of empathy, increasing your emotional intelligence. Instead of finding faults in others, develop a mentality of positive thinking and try to find positive solutions to a particular problem. Remember that all the people you are dealing with are human and we as humans are making mistakes. Moreover, as a human being, we can learn from our mistakes and, by creating a positive attitude, effectively train other people and ourselves to move forward instead of blaming other people or events for mistakes. Be aware that for the success of the game, life requires maintaining a high level of interpersonal communication with your fellow human beings. Most of the time you are helpless without other people helping you. By better understanding your emotional needs, you can communicate with them more effectively and accurately, paving the way for your personal success. In conclusion, emotional intelligence is the ability to understand the emotions of the people around them.

The emotionally intelligent person makes every day of his life a lesson in emotional intelligence. Your goals is to increase your level of emotional intelligence every day while communicating with other people around you. Be smart, follow in the footsteps of smart people, take their lessons, and train among them to gain the wisdom they gain. These are the stereotypical statements of our parents, relatives, retirees and even the office manager. It means being aware and intelligent about the situation. This is the key to discrediting the formula of success. What kind of intelligence are these people talking about? Are you talking about logical intelligence that includes reasoning, recognition patterns, scientific research, decoding of innovative and creative ideas, etc.? Almost 90% of the population has logical intelligence, which is protected by the school / university and the accumulated experience with older people and society. Why do they then fail in life? Stress, tension, bad health, failed relationships are your best friends and over time you also lose self-esteem and confidence in life. It is therefore clear that logical intelligence can be successful to some degree, but saturated after a certain point. Is intelligence really the panacea for all its tensions and suffering? The answer is yes, intelligence with emotions and feelings. It's called emotional intelligence. What is emotional intelligence? Emotional intelligence can also be termed as the ability to perceive emotions, to create and access emotions, and to manage our emotional wealth to promote our personal, professional, and spiritual growth. The benefit is that, if you are fully aware of your emotions and control your actions and reactions, you can motivate and motivate everyone in your environment, develop good relationships and social skills, and express compassion for others. The twentieth century showed the substance of the IQ (Intelligence Quotient), the character of the people was judged on the basis of the intelligent quotient. In a simple language the ability to become a money-lender and to grant to all possible luxurious beings. Various studies have shown that the exercise failed. Emotional intelligence is required to lead a happy, successful, and successful life. Although the intelligent quotient is measured according to certain parameters of mental age and chronological age, emotion has parameters and can be improved at every stage of life.

What are the advantages of EI? It is a false theory that emotional intelligence is only needed in the social sphere to build a long-term quality relationship with others, but it has an important role to play in every aspect of life. The main advantages of emotional intelligence are: - Stress Busters - In our annual emotional intelligence certification, we attach great importance to explaining the importance of emotional intelligence to reduce stress, anxiety and tension and achieve better health. Ability to deal positively with errors and criticisms - There is less praise and more criticism in life. An EI includes its strengths and areas to work on. Less mistakes and criticism are a step towards success. We all know general intelligence (IQ). How many of us know about Emotional Intelligence (EQ)? Emotional intelligence is the ability to identify, use, empathize and positively manage emotions to communicate effectively, understand others, overcome challenges, alleviate stress and resolve conflicts intelligently. To achieve success and happiness in life, emotional intelligence and intellectual capacity (IQ) are required.

Emotional intelligence is useful in work, relationships, career development and personal goals. From now on, we will call EQ Emotional Intelligence. How do you increase the EQ? You can improve your EQ by learning and mastering some key skills: first of all, it is important to understand that your emotions influence different aspects of your daily life - how you carry yourself, how you behave and how you interact with yourself with others. With a high EQ, you will be able to recognize your emotional state and that of others. This understanding helps you communicate and convince others to come closer to you. The success with which you can use your equalizer leads to success in every phase of your life, which leads to greater satisfaction in life.

THE QUALITIES OF EMOTIONAL INTELLIGENCE

There are four feature of emotional intelligence: "Knowing yourself is the beginning of all wisdom. This wisdom holds the key to the further development of your EQ. Self-knowledge: Have you ever stopped thinking about who you really are? Are you good or bad, smart or boring, funny or serious, etc.? Well, if you sit in one place and look like a stranger, you can understand the true "you". If you look closely, you can understand why you acted in a certain way under certain circumstances. Self-observation ability is self-knowledge. Self-knowledge helps you to identify your thoughts, actions, feelings, values, fears, shortcomings, strengths, and generally the entire "you." You can not only turn to yourself, but also to your loved ones and friends to make yourself understood. You can get comments from those who share their honest opinions about you. This helps, to some extent, how others perceive you. In marketing, this is done via a questionnaire about the product and the performance of a company. This is evaluated and used to improve the company's products and services. In the same way, you could ask your loves ones to rate you, and based on their answers you could understand and improve your EQ in those areas where you lacks. As an adult, you can do this exercise daily. In fact, writing a journal is a great way to recognize your true self and your true feelings. If you have a high EQ, you are more focused on your own feelings. This in turn increases your self-confidence in life, in dealing with yourself and others. Self-management: Self-confidence leads to self-management. Self-administration is about controlling your emotions and actions. They control themselves from impulsive behaviors. They develop openness, adaptability, success and optimism. How do you react to certain situations? Do you react or react to people and situations? There is a small difference between these two words, but in practice there is a big difference in meaning. Reaction play an important role in balancing. For example, are you impatient to wait in a long queue on a busy day with very slow traffic? Do you ring other drivers and listen out loud or wait patiently until the traffic is clear? Does it react to heavy traffic? When you are impatient, you are emotionally responsive to the traffic. When you react, you tend to lose your mind. If you shows patience, you reacts and is therefore more understanding and thoughtful. After all, the traffic has to progress sometime!

Self-management means adaptability, transparency, success and optimism. Social Awareness: Your self-awareness and self-management lead you to the next step of social awareness. They are open to understanding the needs, emotions and concerns of others. They can receive emotional signals, feel socially relaxed and recognize the power play in a group or organization. To develop your EQ, you need to see and feel others in their shoes. It is said that people with excellent social awareness tend to be service-minded, empathetic and have organizational awareness. These are the main features of social awareness. The best social conscience is to give people a natural answer, taking their situation and needs into account as much as possible. If you have these characteristics, you can expect your EQ to be high. Relationship Management: The last area you need to develop to improve your EQ is relationship management. We can consider this feature in relation to your job. This is the aspect of your EQ that enables you to inspire other people and help them reach their full potential. It is also important to negotiate successfully, resolve conflicts and work towards a common goal with others. Your success in this last area is directly related to your success in the other three areas, as management is to interact successfully with other people. Is not it an efficient management to get the job done.

A SUCCESSFUL RELATIONSHIP MANAGEMENT

Leadership: Develop others by identifying their strengths. Probably influence others by your own motivation.

- Communication: be a catalyst for change, to embrace new ideas when change is needed

- Conflict Management: connect to people through networks

- Teamwork and collaboration: Everyone can look forward to their own contribution. How does emotional intelligence affect your life? Performance at work: EQ helps you to manage the social complexities of the workplace comfortably, to motivate and manage others and to make your career successful.

Current companies consider emotional intelligence to be an important aspect and carry out balancing tests before hiring. Physical well-being: Stress is in today's world, no matter what profession you belong. Stress is a family factor that causes serious health problems for most people. It is known that the level of uncontrolled stress increases the risk of heart disease. At high stress, our immune system suffers. Mental well-being: Stress has a negative effect on mental health. You may have read or heard about stressed people who commit suicide. If you cannot handle your emotions, it's becomes the victim of mood swings or other mental disorders that rarely allow you to build or sustain strong relationships in life.

Personal Relationships: Understanding your feelings helps you to express your feelings towards your loved ones. When communication is blocked, your relationships suffer both at work and in your private life. Here are six tips to increase your emotional intelligence: Learn to reduce negative emotions. Stay cool and manage stress. Be self-confident and express difficult emotions when needed. Stay proactive and do not react in difficult situations. Recover from adversity. Express intimate emotions in close and personal relationships. You can see to integrate them into your daily life. Emotional Intelligence (EQ) is an art developed in these times to intelligently address your emotions in any life situation. This ability paves the way for success and complacency in every area of your life. Over the past two decades, we've found that our HR capabilities have changed from primary to strategic decisions about the future direction of our business. A key component of this new role is the identification and strategic direction of our talents. The importance of this responsibility cannot be emphasized enough, but how do we find the right people? In the past, recruitment and promotions were based on the applicant's technical skills or education and experience. If someone has the necessary skills and experience, you should be a good leader and share your knowledge with others.

Emotional intelligence focuses on four key factors that successful executives must have: perception of emotions, emotional thinking, understanding of emotions and dealing with emotions. Perception of emotions: This is the ability to recognize the emotions of others. It's about reading to others and understanding their verbal and non-verbal cues. Arguing with emotion: This factor implies the ability to decide what to look for and what to ignore. Understanding Emotions: This means understanding what triggers an emotional reaction in others as well as in yourself. What brings people to work? Emotion Management: This is possibly the most important aspect of emotional intelligence. It's about using feelings in oneself and others to achieve the desired goal. Humans are emotional beings. Knowing how to use these emotions to achieve positive results is a big part of the success of a leader. Emotional intelligence is excellent, and you need more people with high IE. How do you achieve this? Setting this goal is the first and most important step. Here are some ways you can quickly integrate EI into the structure of your existing business. Hiring High EI Employees, The easiest way to change the culture of your business is to recruit new employees. In a successful company there will always be a rotation that can be seen as an opportunity to improve the corporate culture. During the interview process, you can focus on hiring new employees with a high Emotional intelligence.

Use the interview to examine a candidate's emotional response to stressful situations. Make certain that the candidate is being specific. Do not let them get by with just a general response. Assess Your Current Employees Hiring is one way to increase the Emotional Intelligence of your company, but you cannot simply terminate everyone and start from scratch. Your company already has a staff in place. This means assessing your employees with an eye toward EI. Several tests that measure EI are available. The instrument is not as important as the act of measuring and expecting EI. The tool is not as important as measuring and anticipating the EI. The act itself sends the message that this is important in your company now. It also helps you identify those who are suitable for a larger role in your business. Emphasize how the results are achieved and not the results themselves: the results are relevant. You want your employees to behave well, but the methods they use to achieve these results are also fundamental. Your employees need to know. Be sure to emphasize the importance of communication, teamwork and flexibility in conducting your assessments. Promote the Right People When it comes time to fill a position within the company through promotion, make sure that you promote people who demonstrate a high level of EI. Before promoting, you should ask the candidates pointed questions about what they think it takes to be effective in their new position. Then, ask them how they have demonstrated those skills in their current positions. Once again, by stressing EI in the promotion process, you are sending a message to the rest of your company that these are valuable traits. Emotional Intelligence is a predictor of success. Regardless of the industry you are in, focusing on emotional intelligence and technical skills will help you grow your business. Employee productivity has improved and employee retention has increased.

A business with a high EI rate is a great place to work, and talented employees will not want to leave. Companies that retain high-performing employees are successful. As a HR professional, you strive to help the other members of your company reach their full potential. You know that by doing so your company will continue to grow and succeed. Implementing programs that emphasize Emotional Intelligence is one way to accomplish those goals. There are a host of programs that will help you increase your company's overall intelligence.

WHY YOU NEED TO INCREASE YOUR EMOTIONAL INTELLIGENCE

The most important aspect for increasing the emotional intelligence in your company is your commitment. Once employees realize that EI is important to the business and its overall success, they will look for opportunities for improvement. All that is required of you is to lay the foundation. Emotional intelligence, also known as IE, is the innate ability of a person to perceive, evaluate, and influence the emotions and emotions of others in their environment.

Emotional intelligence is divided into five parts:

1. Self-knowledge: The ability and the need to understand one's own emotions, to know them and to recognize those feelings.

2. Demand Management: It is the ability to deal with emotions in a way relevant to the current situation.

3. Self-motivation: The ability to remain focused on one goal despite your doubt and impulsiveness.

4. Empathy: The ability to engage with the feelings of others and to understand them effectively as they understand themselves.

5. Relationship Management: The ability to handle conflict negotiation and mediation by third parties.

Why is emotional intelligence important?

Although emotional intelligence lacks the scope of quantitative empirical cognitive research at IQ, research in the field of cognitive learning suggests that emotional intelligence is a fundamental key aspect of learning. According to a journal or research by the National center for Children's Hospital programs, a student's success in learning new materials is due to his or her individual level of confidence, self-control, curiosity, communication skills, collaboration, euphoria, and self-confidence. Intentionality all of these features are aspects of emotional intelligence. More recently, social scientists have begun to discover the relationship of emotional intelligence with other organizational psychologies, such as: B .: Leadership, group performance, individual performance, interpersonal exchange, performance evaluation and change management. Man is a social being and our success in dealing with people is closely linked to our emotional intelligence.

Improve your emotional intelligence. Researchers and scientists see the intelligence quotient, also known as I.Q. known to be fixed, which means that it does not change throughout life. EI is very different from I.Q. in this E.I. It can be improved through a combination of life experience, maturity, mindset and perseverance. You can improve your emotional intelligence by following these steps:

1. Think about the last moment you can think of when you hurt someone's feelings, and analyze what your reactions were at that point in time, and analyze what you said and what the other person did emotionally Has caused pain. Try putting yourself in the other place and empathize with yourself and your feelings by saying those words. In this exercise, you will effectively improve your understanding of empathy, increasing your emotional intelligence. 2. Instead of finding faults in others, develop a mentality of positive thinking and try to find positive solutions to a specific problem. Remember that all the people you are dealing with are human and we as humans are making mistakes. Moreover, as a human being, we can learn from our mistakes and, by creating a positive attitude, effectively train other people and ourselves to move forward instead of blaming other people or events for mistakes.

3. Realize that a high level of interpersonal communication with your fellow human beings is required to succeed in the game called life. Most of the time it is helpless without other people helping you. By better understanding your emotional needs, you can communicate

with them more effectively and accurately, paving the way for your personal success.

In summary, emotional intelligence is the ability to understand one's own emotions and those of those around them. The emotionally intelligent person makes a lesson in emotional intelligence every day of his life and his goal is to increase his emotional intelligence every day as he communicates with other people in his environment and himself. Be smart, follow the footsteps of intelligent people, take their insights and train among them so that you can also grasp the wisdom they get. These are the stereotyped statements of our parents, relatives, elders and even the head of the office. It means being aware and intelligent of the situation in order to expose the formula for success. We speak of logical intelligence, which includes thought, pattern recognition, scientific inquiry, the decoding of innovative and creative ideas and so on. Almost 90% of the population has logical intelligence, a spoon defended by the school / university and experiences gathered with the elderly and society. Why do they fail in life? Stress, tension, ill health, failed relationships are their best friends and over time they lose self-esteem and confidence in life. So it is obvious that logical intelligence can guide the performance diagram to some extent, but saturate after a certain point. Is intelligence really the panacea for all your tensions and suffering? The answer is yes, intelligence with emotions and feelings. It's called emotional intelligence.

ALL ABOUT EMOTIONAL INTELLIGENCE

Be smart, follow in the footsteps of intelligent people, absorb their insights and train them emotions, to create and access emotions, and to manage our emotional wealth to promote our personal, professional, and spiritual growth. The benefit is that, if you are fully aware of your emotions and control your actions and reactions, you can motivate and motivate everyone in your environment, develop good relationships and social skills, and express compassion for others. The twentieth century showed the substance of the IQ (Intelligence Quotient), the character of the people was judged on the basis of the intelligent quotient. In a simple language the ability to become a money-lender and to grant to all possible luxurious beings. Various studies have shown that the exercise failed. Emotional intelligence is required to lead a happy, successful, and successful life. Although the intelligent quotient is measured under certain parameters of mental age and chronological age, emotional intelligence has no such parameters and can be improved at every stage of life. It is a false theory that emotional intelligence is only needed in the social field, such as developing a long-term quality relationship with others, but it plays an important role in all aspects of life. The key benefits of emotional intelligence are:

Stress Reduction: In our annual certification of Emotional Intelligence, we attach great importance to explaining the importance of Emotional Intelligence to reduce stress, anxiety and tension and to achieve better health.

Ability to deal with mistakes and criticism positively: There is less praise and more criticism in life. An EI includes its strengths and the areas in which it must work. Bankruptcy and criticism are just one step to success. We all know General Intelligence (IQ). How many of us are familiar with Emotional Intelligence (EQ)? Emotional intelligence is the ability to identify, use, empathize, and positively manage emotions in order to communicate effectively, to understand others, to master challenges, to reduce stress, and to resolve conflicts intelligently. Since then, it has become a buzzword in the fields of psychology and sociology. The modules and the transversal skills trainers emphasize the importance of emotional intelligence in the workplace and in social environments. Achieving success and happiness in life requires both emotional intelligence and intellectual capacity (IQ). Emotional intelligence is useful at work, in relationships, in career development, and in personal goals. From now on we will call EQ Emotional Intelligence. How do you increase your EQ? You can improve your EQ by learning and mastering some key competences: First, it is important that you understand that your emotions affect different aspects of your daily life: the way you behave.

Self-management: Self-confidence leads to self-management. Self-administration is about controlling your emotions and actions. They control themselves from impulsive behaviors. They develop openness, adaptability, success and optimism. How do you react to certain situations? Do you react or react to people and situations? There is a small difference between these two words, but in practice there is a big difference in meaning. Reaction play an important role in balancing. When you react, you tend to lose your mind.

Social Awareness: Your self-awareness and self-management lead you to the next step of social awareness. They are open to understanding the needs, emotions and concerns of others. They can receive emotional signals, feel socially relaxed and recognize the power play in a group or organization. It is said that people with excellent social awareness tend to be service-minded, empathetic and have organizational awareness. These are the main features of social awareness. The best social conscience is to give people a natural answer, taking their situation and needs into account as much as possible. If you have these characteristics, you can expect your EQ to be high.

Relationship Management: The last area you need to develop to improve your EQ is relationship management. We can consider this feature in relation to your job. This is the aspect of your EQ that enables you to inspire other people and help them reach their full potential. It is also important to negotiate successfully, resolve conflicts and work towards a common goal with others. Your success in this last area is directly related to your success in the other three areas, as management is to interact successfully with other people. Is not it an efficient management to get the job done?

How does emotional intelligence affect your life?

Performance at work: EQ helps you to manage the social complexities of the workplace comfortably, to motivate and manage others and to make your career successful. Current companies consider emotional intelligence to be an important aspect and carry out balancing tests before hiring.

Physical well-being: Stress is in today's world, no matter what profession you belong. Stress is a family factor that causes serious health problems for most people. It is known that the level of uncontrolled stress increases the risk of heart disease. At high stress, our immune system suffers.

Perception of emotions: This is the ability to recognize the emotions of others. It's about reading to others and understanding their verbal and non-verbal cues.

Argument emotion: This factor implies the ability to decide what to look for and what to ignore.

Understanding Emotions: This means understanding what triggers an emotional reaction in others as well as in yourself. What brings people to work.

Emotion Management: This is possibly the most important aspect of emotional intelligence. It's about using feelings in oneself and others to achieve the desired goal. Humans are emotional beings. Knowing how to use these emotions to achieve positive results is a big part of the success of a leader.

Since its introduction to the business world, the impact of Emotional Intelligence has been tested in clinical and real-world environments. Every time it happened with great success. High EI employees have a positive, negative impact on their environment and are better employees. Companies with a large number of emotionally intelligent employees are more successful than companies with a comparatively small number of emotionally intelligent employees.

This does not mean that companies should hug each morning. Employees with a high IE have also been shown to have greater technical capacity. They use their abilities and the abilities of others more effectively than those with a low EI. It is possible to continue to focus on technical capacities, but to involve EI when it is time to recruit, dismiss and promote staff. Okay, emotional intelligence is excellent and you need more people with high IE. How do you achieve this? Setting this goal is the first and most important step. Here are some ways you can quickly integrate EI into the structure of your existing business. Promote the Right People When it comes to occupying a position within the company through sponsorship, you should definitely encourage people with a high level of EI. Before promotion, you should ask the candidates timely how they assess the effectiveness of their new position. Then ask them how they have demonstrated these skills in their current positions. Again, by highlighting EI in the advertising process, you send a message to the rest of your business that these are valuable assets. Emotional intelligence is a success factor. No matter what business you are in, focusing on emotional intelligence and technical skills will help your business grow. Employee productivity is improved and employee retention is increased. A company with a high IE rate is a great place to work, and talented people will not want to leave the company. Companies that hold high-performing employees are successful.

Have you ever seen someone who graduated as the best in his class, who was extremely intelligent and failed again and again in business? And what about the other people with moderate intelligence who literally build empires and change the face of the world?

What about Henry Ford? He never went to high school or college. In fact, Ford left school at fifteen, but he accumulated a fortune and changed the world forever. Perhaps you are wondering how it works and what benefits emotional intelligence has for you and your business. Here is the deal. Happiness has absolutely nothing to do with standard intelligence, but with the so-called Emotional Intelligence (IE). According to Merriam Webster, emotional intelligence describes "the ability or, in the case of the trait, to identify, assess and manage the emotions of oneself, others and groups".

Emotional intelligence is, in simple terms, the ability to recognize, understand and work with one's emotions and emotions. Other benefits of emotional intelligence include a higher level of intuition, compassion, empathy and the ability to successfully analyze these emotions. Because business relationships are business relationships, these factors can influence or influence the success of a small business owner. For example, a negotiation often requires the ability to listen, understand where a person is coming from, put themselves in their place, and then find a creative solution that leads to a win-win situation for both sides. This cannot be achieved only with the knowledge of the book: it requires emotional intelligence.

Emotional intelligence also helps you understand, anticipate, and control the expectations of your fellow human beings. This is useful in dealing with customers, potential customers, suppliers, business partners and even employees and contractors. If you can help people around you feel valued, anticipate their expectations, and manage them before they realize it, you're way ahead of the game. For example, if you can see that your audience is longing for affiliation, and hope or expect your business to help them behave that way, you can develop strategies to address this. The benefits of emotional intelligence in business management are too numerous to name. Here are some more for your consideration. Wondering where it fits? What are you doing well and where can you improve yourself?

* Manage conflicts better * Faster solve problems * Improve customer service * Hire the best people for the job * Trust your business instincts and intuition * Listen to others, understand them, and make them feel appreciated * Control Yours Respond to challenges and stay positive when mistakes occur. * Promote your customers because you can empathize with them better. * Write better, content more emotional. * Connect with potential partners and build business relationships.

HOW TO INCREASE YOUR EMOTIONAL INTELLIGENCE

Many people think that their intelligence level, whether standard IQ or emotional intelligence, is something that they were born with and that cannot be improved. That's just not true! All you need to do is to improve your emotional intelligence and I have the desire to do so. Be aware of how people behave, how you behave and how you react, and try to replace others. Learning empathy is perhaps the best way to strengthen one's emotional intelligence, and it makes a big difference in how one does business.

Take some time to analyze your relationships based on the many benefits of emotional intelligence listed in this article. Follow your own progress. You could even spend a week on each factor you want to improve. You can do it, and since the benefits of emotional intelligence are so important to your business success, it would start immediately! To increase your emotional intelligence, you must be aware of the emotions that you experience at a particular time, and you also need to be concerned with the emotions that you have suppressed to avoid dealing with them. It is a common tendency to reject a certain emotion or to convince oneself that you are not experiencing a particular emotion because it is unpleasant or for whatever reason the emotion appears inappropriate under the circumstances. Emotional intelligence requires that you know and handle your own emotions. You can not do that automatically, it's a process. To successfully complete this process, it is helpful to remember the following facts about your emotions: Emotional intelligence is based on emotional awareness.

Emotional intelligence differs from regular or classical intelligence in that it can enhance your emotional intelligence at will. Being emotionally intelligent is an essential part of building close relationships with family, friends, and employees. People with high emotional intelligence are valued because they are constant, calm, and secure, and seem to have the innate ability to understand others. They always seem to know what to do in a given situation, because their emotions do not overwhelm them, so they can think more clearly and act more rationally. Emotions are constantly changing. Being aware of your feelings and what triggers them is not the same as stopping them. Notice how the different things you do on a given day causes one emotion to develop and another to wane, and you'll find that emotions can always change.

Your emotions are often associated with physical sensations. You've probably noticed that the way your body responds to the emotions of fear is different from the emotion of happiness, and that you feel physically happy when you're happy, unlike when it's angry and so on. For example, if you're careful that your hands are shaking, your muscles are tense and that your heart is beating rapidly, all of which are tied to being afraid, will help you realize why you are afraid and will help you manage that fear so that you can handle it constructively.

Emotional intelligence does not replace reason and logic. Being aware of the emotions and feelings you are experiencing and knowing how to deal with those emotions and feelings becomes essentially automatic. As soon as you no longer instinctively struggle with your emotions and feelings, your thinking and thinking skills are clearer and more precise and you can use them to overcome your emotions without being overcome by them. Like everything else, you will improve this by practicing, and doing more practice. When we understand our feelings, what they are and how they affect us, we create the basics to become aware of ourselves. Self-management then continues with a range of other skills that help us to increase our emotional intelligence.

For many people, 2019 began with a promise that we will achieve what we have missed last year. It's often the most difficult things to do: manage your schedule, treat people the way you should, and keep perspective when chaos is near. The reality is that almost 80% of us will fall out of the backup car on Super Bowl Sunday; and by next year, only 5% of us will have achieved our goals. There are two reasons why we are so mean to achieve our intentions. The first is that we bite more than we can chew. It may seem reasonable to acquire three or four new skills to expand your repertoire, but that is an expectation that the mind can not perform. If we try to develop several new skills at once, they will be discouraging and overburdening with competitive priorities that distract us. The second reason why most self-improvement efforts are doomed to failure is that our emotions have the uncomfortable habit of abducting our behavior. Without strong ability to recognize and manage our emotions, old habits will surely fade.

The good news is that you can address both issues and make the changes you want by developing a single Emotional Intelligence (EQ) this year. Research conducted in the past two decades has shown that emotional intelligence is probably the strongest success factor ever discovered, and that it affects all areas of work performance and annual income up to mood and satisfaction living Emotional intelligence includes most of the other critical ones Skills, including time management, decision making and communication. It is not surprising that emotional intelligence accounts for 58% of performance in all types of jobs and is the single largest driver of leadership and personal excellence. But how does emotional intelligence play such an important role in so many important skills?

Emotions are the root of all human behavior. Regardless of whether we are aware or not, the motivation behind every action (however small) is inherently emotional. When you master emotional intelligence, you have the ability to understand and control the motivations of your behavior. As you work to improve your emotional intelligence, you improve your skills in a number of other important skills as EQ reaches the heart of the matter. Emotional intelligence is powerful and efficient: you can focus your energy in one direction only to achieve tremendous results. The following five skills illustrate some of the huge gains you can only make if you increase your emotional intelligence.

1. Time Management: Protect Your Most Valuable Resources In this time of abundance, time is the only thing that nobody has enough. Few people realize how time management depends on the emotional intelligence skills of self-management and relationship management. Creating a good schedule is very rational, but adhering to this schedule is extremely emotional. Many of us start every day with the best intentions to handle their time wisely. But then we receive a complicated e-mail from a colleague, a phone call from a friend, or we redirect until our plans catch fire. We spent the rest of the day extinguishing someone else's fire or solving problems that were not there in the morning. Before you realize, the day is over and you do not have hours left. If the distractions are yours, following a schedule requires self-government. When the needs of others to try their plans it takes a great deal of social awareness and relationship management to finesse the relationship while ensuring that your priorities are still addressed.

2. Tolerance to change: Stay flexible in the face of the only guarantee in life. Show so many people who says they loves change, and also show others a well-intentioned liar. Change is sometimes uncomfortable for everyone and for many of us it always causes our skin to crawl. Those who use well-tolerated self-esteem and self-management skills tolerate change much more successfully than others. Self-confidence allows you to easily adapt to change, giving you the perspective you need to see when changes come and when changes can be made. Self-government keeps you informed at the moment, often with the reminder that even the most stable and reliable aspects of your life are not completely under your control. People who are reluctant to change, who have a high degree of self-confidence and self-management, even spend a little time each week to list possible changes and the actions they can take.

3. Presentation skills: Meet your audience with a positive conversation. Few things cause fear in the heart of the average person, such as to be the center of attention in a crowded room (your heart accelerates, right?). Emotional intelligence not only alerts you to your emotions, but also equips you with strategies to prevent you from being arrested.

4. Decision Making: How Emotions Make Rational Decisions It took too long for the world to become aware of the fact that emotions in choices can and should simply not be ignored. The neurosciences now show us that sometimes it is the most rational thing to trust in your feelings when deciding. For this to work, you need to be aware of the feelings of why you have them and how they affect the situation. There is no substitute for the core competencies of emotional intelligence, self-esteem and self-control.

5. Assertiveness: mastering the art of letting it have Emotional intelligence is often mistaken as a synonym for "nice". In fact, the most emotionally intelligent answer is often one in which he expresses his feelings directly and openly. To rewrite Aristotle, to become angry is easy. To become angry at the right person at the right time and to the right degree requires emotional intelligence. Emotional intelligence does not allow you to beat or become the doormat of another person. To be assertive, you need to know what you are feeling (self-confidence), read the other party carefully (social awareness), and express yourself to get the best results (self-management and relationship management). Of course, people with high equalizers do so.

Often the question arises as to whether people with a high EQ can be born or whether they can be learned. We all know people who seem to have a natural gift for how well they work with others. They intuitively understand how to reassure people and, if they are leaders, motivate their employees and actively involve them in their work. The truth is that some people are more naturally gifted than others, but the good news is that you can learn balance skills. Clear research has been done on this and there is good evidence that people can learn to interact more effectively at work. But to do that, people need to be personally motivated and to practice what they learn at work and to strengthen themselves for their new abilities. Most of us can think of people who seem to have a natural ability to work well with others. While EQ can be an important talent, can it be developed or is it something that a person is born with? There are research findings that clearly show that EQ can be learned. The good news for the business is that although there is a genetic predisposition to emotional intelligence, those skills can develop and remain long-term. There is certainly a need for exercise and empowerment to develop these skills. And finally, the balancing abilities will not improve without the sincere desire to do so.

CAN EMOTIONAL INTELLIGENCE BE LEARN?

While compensation is relevant in almost every work situation in which people work together, using the compensation to improve leadership and management performance is of great interest to the human resources community. In today's challenging economy, everyone is trying to increase productivity with fewer resources. It is this desire for high performance that prompted Sales Training to deal deeper into EQ. We are constantly helping companies achieve greater performance through training and development of interpersonal skills. Our experience with companies of all sizes shows that effective leaders can improve the performance of their organizations. Certainly, different situations require different leadership techniques. In practice, a leader with good gender equality skills can assess a situation and determine an appropriate response. Without EQ, a person with a high IQ, experience and good ideas will not be a great leader. And the higher a leader progresses, the more important the emotional intelligence becomes. However, the potential for compensation problems is also increasing with senior executives. Compensation and Leadership are criticism of emotional intelligence that we often hear that its sounds good in theory, but hard to put into practice. And some of the EQ advocates do not seem to be very good at examining what it looks like in the daily workplace or how it can be practiced and improved. One of the real problems here is that emotional intelligence is more general in its approach. It is assumed that all people can show these abilities more or less the same. Less recognize that not all effective leaders have all of the balancing capabilities, and that the value of the compensation is largely situation-dependent: in some situations more equalization skills are needed than in others. What is always overlooked however is the fact that another dimension of behavior that affects how people act and how they interpret the behavior of others.

Balance and versatility in today's economy, businesses are looking for ways to improve their productivity. Emotional intelligence has become a resource to improve the performance of people and their organizations. And as research further documents, EQ makes a difference. EQ brings objective and measurable benefits, including increased sales, recruitment and retention, and more effective leadership. There is also evidence that compensation skills can be developed through training programs. Versatility training teaches specific skills that enhance emotional intelligence. Developing this experience makes people and their organizations more productive and effective.

The results were consistent in all countries and cultures. Emotional intelligence was the variable in each of these examples. In recent years, the interest in emotional intelligence (EQ) has increased as research has shown that they have an impact on a variety of commercial activities. These include the recruitment and selection of jobs, sales results and leadership performance.

"1. Emotional Intelligence (EQ) Your brain controls your mood and your ability to manage stress and respond to challenges, control your ability to read other people's emotions and respond appropriately, your emotional intelligence or your EQ. It is the aspect of brain fitness that has a major impact on your self-esteem, your everyday mood and your success in the social environment, including professional and family life, has cortical-limbic being responsible for controlling your emotional intelligence and how most systems in your brain can Improve these with a specific approach. "The first emotional intelligence capability that restores, feeds, trains, relaxes, and brings new learning experiences to your brain.

EMOTIONAL INTELLIGENCE HAPPENS INTERNALLY AND EXTERNALLY

Once the brain is fit, we can start discussing the discrete capabilities of emotional intelligence. Again, we have to work on ourselves first, with the internal dialogue. As a domestic violence teacher, we work with people who are not dedicated to emotional intelligence or who do not know how to do it, and at first teach basic internal dialogue skills. Remember, you do not have to agree or disagree, just listen, maybe even turn your head to the side and listen. Why do you have to do this frequently? Because the reaction of human orientation quickly moves it away. We are ready to respond to the movement in the environment, and when you look at the window, where only a flash of light was seen, you can forget the commitment you have made and take part in the discussion, as very healthy brain processes data at a rate.

Change your thoughts quickly. The next capacity of emotional intelligence you need to address is to deal with your own feelings. This implies the awareness that thoughts change feelings. So when you feel uncomfortable, you have to change the mind to change the feeling, take a deep breath, or do your biofeedback of heart rate variability. Again, work on the personal aspects of emotional intelligence so that you can act effectively, cooperatively, and in partnership in the external relationship. The term emotional intelligence, abbreviated as EI, has something to do with the ability to highlight, evaluate, and handle other people's emotions and emotions.

The conflicting proposals for defining and using emotional intelligence in the various areas of interest are still in focus. Regardless of the different definition and use of the concept of emotional intelligence on specific topics that are considered purely technical, the etymology of the term can be found in a work particularly the relevance of the emotional expression for existence or survival and second adaptation, Both with the definition of the concept of emotional intelligence; Now let's examine how the emotional intelligence of an individual can be improved. It is remarkably empirical that people with high EI have greater and better chances of success in all areas of life. Before you begin the emotional intelligence test, you should consider some of the principles that are useful for improving a person's EI. It of high assurance that after concluding this chapter, all ideas contained in this document will be included in the readers' own ideas.

1) Homage - This word is not simply a sequence of linguistic symbols associated with sounds, and conveys a meaning. It is more than what is described in dictionaries and encyclopedias. It is not something that can be gained by drastic means, but it can be achieved over time. This is still an empty concept, unless people manifest it to others. Respect is a solid foundation for the development of EI. If you want others to respect you, you must first learn to respect their feelings or emotions. In this way a mutual respect is built up. The golden rule emphasizes that "to do to others what others should do to you". Irrespective of the problem, if your office partner has big problems, you should show empathy and compassion and try to find workable solutions that can alleviate your problem. If your friend has a different belief because of his religious affiliations, try not to engage in a religious conversation that may offend him. Silence is sometimes the best way to show respect.

2) Using the Reverse Psychology Technique Of course - there are times when things get difficult or rude and happiness is not on your side. Just rest when you're angry and not in a good mood. Try to find your way around a difficult situation. Why not try to paint a real smile every time you encounter a problem. Do not Worry Remember that having a seat in a rocking chair is like sitting, even though they move you, but you do not take them everywhere. And if you are worried,

this will by no means lead to a day in your life, but it will only do the opposite. So why worry if your problem just gets worse?

3) Listening to wars in history could have been avoided if only all the leaders of the nations had learned to listen to each other's different views and then try to come up with plans that might erase those differences. Learn to listen and listen to learn. Most successful people are not loquacious type of individuals, but rather they are the kind of folks who love to listen to other people's brilliant ideas and learn from them. Listening is one of the factors contributing to their sustainable success. It can be said that when you constantly listen and learn to apply the good ideas that you have listened to or have given an ear to, then you will become very much successful in everything you do.

The above steps to improve your emotional intelligence are easy to understand. However, recognizing these ideas is just the first important step in helping to make the most of your IE's improvement. The hardest part is living it, which depends entirely on you. A practical combination of interpersonal intelligence and intrapersonal intelligence is called emotional intelligence. This is about summarizing the topic in a simplified form that can be used by parents and teachers. Consider Emotional Intelligence or IE, which give answers to six questions: Question 1 is why emotional intelligence is important? The powerful answer is that a person's emotional intelligence or EI is often the most important factor in the success or failure of a career. Apart from downsizing in a weakened economy, more employees are dismissed or not promoted because they could not develop their EI for any other reason. Parents and teachers who help young people to develop their EI make a wonderful contribution to the future success of young people.

Question 2: What is Emotional Intelligence? It is the ability of a person to deal constructively with their own emotions and the emotions of others, promoting teamwork and productivity rather than conflict. Perhaps most importantly, it is a skill that, like the other intelligences that we will discuss in future articles, can be taught and 'grow'.

Question 3 is, how do you recognize emotional intelligence? The most direct way to answer this is to describe what you will see when a person has a high level of the five basic components of ei. The person will show these abilities:

Of course, the opposite of high IE is not hard to see. If you are exposed to a person who is very emotional, reacts quickly to your feelings, and has little or no sensitivity to the feelings of others; Employee communications often tend to harm or annoy others. With series of organization being motivated and aware of the need for a good teamwork from their employees and earning the goodwill of customers who do not tolerate rudeness, these companies are looking for high-EI workers and training to enhance their emotional intelligence skills to improve existing employee.

How we can develop high emotional intelligence among young people. The optimal period for the development of a strong emotional intelligence is from birth to puberty. This means that both parents and teachers from kindergarten to high school control the time when everything can be done to help a young person develop a strong emotional intelligence. Parents who constructively deal with their own emotions, respect the feelings of their children but consciously encourage their child to recognize how their behaviors affect others, foster the development of the strong. Schools that train employees to continue this growth process and create EI development exercises in existing courses make an important contribution to the students' success potential. Excellent curriculum materials are available to help teachers in this field. How can you promote the teaching of emotional intelligence in your child's school? If you are considering day care programs, ask providers to provide specific information about their EI development activities. If the answers are vague or difficult to answer, look for another program. How Can Your School Promote the Growth of Emotional Intelligence? Students and teachers can: Debate to become fully aware of the power and principles of one. Practicing every day how the power of EI is implemented: in class interactions, in peer discussions, in the cafeteria, at home, everywhere. Rate the post in other to encourage such person and put zeal to perform better next time. Bean more realistic by describing the scales used: Intrapersonal (Self-Regard, Emotional Self Awareness, Assertiveness, Independence, and Self-Actualization); Interpersonal Scales (Empathy, Social Responsibility, Interpersonal Relationship); Adaptability Scales (Reality Testing, Flexibility, Problem Solving); Stress Management Scales (Stress Tolerance, Impulse Control); and General Mood Scales (Optimism, Happiness). The four factors Choose social responsibility, interpersonal relationships, stress tolerance and impulse control.

Social Responsibility At work and in relationships, you have certain choices that you can make. You can behave like a mature, thoughtful, empathetic and responsible person. The willingness to give and take, to understand the other person's point of view, to preserve the perspective and to maintain a broader view and to be generous in your relationships with others, increases harmony and reduces stress in the workplace for you and your colleagues , Interpersonal relationships is not unrealistic to say that there are two types of people in this world: those who give and those who take. When we are involved in marriage counseling, less quickly check which end of the spectrum is the most important personal style of each couple. Of course, if you have two policyholders and no commitment, you have a battlefield where each partner leaves to get as much as possible from the other. If you have a donor and a policyholder, you find a person whose life chances are sacrificed for the selfish interests of others. If you have two donors, you probably have a pleasant, generous, loving relationship: you know you're a winner. In many ways, you can observe the same system in the workplace, where some people struggle with nails and teeth to win at every opportunity. Developing collaborative teams requires people to be sensitive and to build positive, respectful and shared relationships. When these relationships are the dominant interpersonal characteristics of work teams, the work stress for all is reduced.

Stress tolerance, everyone has a different ability to deal with stress and anxiety. Some people, as they say, have a short backup and are unable to withstand even the slightest stress. This is a pain and misery for all around them and they have to endure their limited ability to control stress. We can improve our ability to deal proactively and effectively with stress. We can increase our stress tolerance mechanisms. This requires that we are mature, thoughtful, and indulge in youthful expressions of frustration and impatience. Impulse control helps to reduced ability to control impulses and self-regulatory management as a key feature. Sad enough, there are several workplaces who show reckless disdain even for a small amount of impulse control. They seem to believe that they have an undeniable right to spread their emotional eruptions whenever they want and without regard for others. The opposite of this is the responsible person, who does not increase other people's stress levels, but carefully and effectively deals with the pressure and stress they experience. Interpersonal intelligence is the ability to understand other people: what motivates them, how they work, how they work with them. Successful sellers, politicians, teachers, doctors and religious leaders are probably people with a high level of interpersonal intelligence. Intrapersonal intelligence is the ability to know and understand oneself accurately and truthfully and to use this information effectively for interpersonal relationships as well as for personal growth and development.

HOW CAN WE IMPROVE OUR EQ?

EQ can be developed through practice and learning. Most of us have forgotten to recognize our feelings. We often confuse our thinking with our feelings. So we have distanced ourselves very much from ourselves. The SEQ implies the development of discriminating knowledge: the difference between the perceiver and the perceived, the subject and the object. Identify the emotions of others and our own emotions as separate instead of mixing them as a mutual reaction. There are five main skills in EQ:

1. Self-knowledge: Recognize yourself. Be conscious be aware of our physical, mental and emotional activities. Stay in touch with us. It takes practice to observe ourselves. Once we recognize our emotional state, we can achieve changes that adapt to the situation.

2. Emotional maturity: When we are aware of our inner being, maturity means to give us all dimensions of ourselves without judging. Accept things the way they are. Have the courage to explore and use our blockages to deal constructively with our situations.

3. Self-motivation: taking responsibility for our emotions and actions. Because we know that we do everything, we do it for a reason, and we have the opportunity to do or not to do anything. When we make a choice, we do it to escape the pain and to feel joy. Pain and joy are the two biggest dimensions of motivation. The elimination of pain brings us to great heights and when we have eliminated the pain, we can approach the addition of pleasure. That's our biggest motivation.

4. Empathic Understanding: Leaving your own frame, entering the mental model of others and looking at it completely from the perspective of others. Understand others and communicate the understanding in the other's language, and receive confirmation of that understanding rather than adding its own meaning.

5. Quality communication: active listening to convey empathy and understanding. Understand before you want to be understood.

How do YOU use EQ in difficult conversations?

We can develop some general principles for difficult conversations where the equalizer plays a very important role in making the conversations beneficial to both sides.

1. Explain your own purpose and intention. Self-awareness and emotional maturity can help us clarify our purpose. Wondering why you want to have this conversation? If your intention is one-sided that someone agrees with you or supports you, you probably have a very defensive reaction. If you really want to evolve, you can curiously enter the conversation to explore the situation and check the accuracy of your views. Knowing your own purpose and intention teaches you how to productively change your own behavior before you affect the other. Self-knowledge helps you to clarify your intention and purpose.

In any difficult conversation, it's really about three things: what really happened, how you feel about it, what happened, and what the situation says about your identity. Get in contact with your emotions and feelings to know your fears and your important issues. In this way, you can review your assumptions and attributions and validate your data. Some questions to assess your emotional maturity: - Are you sympathetic to everyone? – Are you open and curious or do you come with preconceived ideas? Are you ready to learn? – Are you transparent in sharing everything you know? – Are you completely committed to the result? - What are your worst fears? What are your deepest wishes? - Do you take responsibility for your contributions?

2. Build a conversation basis. Agreeing with the other person on the purpose of the conversation: What do you want to talk about? What is your interest in provoking this conversation? Without this, the other person is more likely to continue their own conclusions and become defensive, which does not allow them to submit their proposal. Self-motivation is the quality that will help you the most as you know that you have this option as an option, even if its difficult. By using the effectiveness of empathy and understanding, one can make it clear

to the other person that this is not just a one-way conversation, but should be discussed for mutual benefit. You can create the base in the following four steps:

- Do not just say what happened in your opinion, but ask others as well. Talk about how the other feels, and share how you feel. Present your interests after clarifying the needs and interests of each other.

3. Focus on the common design process; usually, in difficult conversations, we go back to the history of the situation and lose track of future goals as they were designed together. This in turn requires self-awareness and emotional maturity to be authentic, to recognize where the process is derailed and to focus on the process. It also requires self-motivation to continue until the end of the process. Old data is often flawed because our reasoning is flawed when we are afraid of a situation or frustrated by a relationship. The self-motivated approach will help us stay in the present and make progress in the future.

4. I agree to monitor and discuss progress again. Success in difficult situations is achieved if you do something else. Since this is a behavioral change, it is necessary to coordinate intentions with actions. Always agree to monitor progress and celebrate success after difficult conversations.

By improving the emotional intelligence (EI) "The Wave of Conscious Solutions" and "Spirituality in Business." As we welcome this new era and embrace the widespread adoption of business-savvy techniques, make sure your organization is one of the first to introduce it and benefit from the advantages over your competitors that lag behind the traditional business principles. Emotional intelligence, a conscious solution to reactionary emotional habits, is the ability to acquire and apply knowledge about their emotions and the emotions of others. Information about what you feel helps you to make effective decisions about what you say or do (or what you do not say or do).

You can use your feelings to make better decisions now and to better control yourself and your impact on others. The concept of emotional intelligence is based on brain research, which shows that these abilities differ from technical and purely cognitive abilities because they affect another part of the brain: the emotional center, the limbic system. Emotional intelligence consists of five basic skills. The first is to know how you feel. The second is to deal with your feelings, especially stressful ones. The third is self-motivation, the fourth is empathy and the fifth is relationship management.

The business case - Emotional intelligence skills have proven to be critical to individual and organizational success. Emotional intelligence research has revealed that the impact is profound and involves a variety of business / personal issues, including more creativity and innovation, higher productivity, better decision-making, and higher profits. The economic argument for developing emotional intelligence becomes clear when we realize that the emotions that executives, employees, and customers feel have an impact on decision-making, mental clarity, and the bottom line of business, as well as the effectiveness of governments and organizations without they have a profit The emotions that leaders experience affect the overall climate and culture of an organization. In particular, the emotions of leaders influence what employees feel, how satisfied they are, how loyal they are, and how productive and efficient they are. In turn, the way employees feel and do their jobs affects how customers feel, how satisfied they are with products and services, and how loyal a customer ultimately is to the company or organization. And how loyal the customers are has a direct impact on a company's bottom line and profitability. Remember that the fundamental element in this set of relationships is leadership. Managers are not just CEO or Executive Vice President or Director. The responsible person in each team, manager and person in the organization is a leader. Self-leadership is one of the most important factors in focusing on skills development.

Self-management is the internal ability to guide oneself to make the best decisions at any time of the day, both at work and at home.

Negative effects on the business

Examining the effects of unmanaged emotional responses and lack of emotional intelligence skills shows that this has a significant and negative impact on the business. Uncontrolled emotional reactions or lack of emotional intelligence of managers and employees at all levels can lead to a lack of innovation and creativity. This what unmanaged emotional responses cause -

Decreased productivity, or decrease customer satisfaction and loyalty or professional derailment or high rotation or stagnant change initiatives or decline in income or increased costs for stress and health care or negative organizational climate / cultural violence in the workplace development of emotional intelligence skills.

The best part is that you can also learn emotional intelligence skills. However, there is one caveat: If we use the typical training approach to improve analytical or technical skills, we are doomed to failure. Traditional programs do not take into account the factors by which the limbic system (emotional center of the brain) best learns: motivation, extended practice, and feedback. The development of emotional intelligence requires that people eliminate old behaviors and adopt new ones. And this requires practice and self-reflection about the impact of using new skills.

EMOTIONAL INTELLIGENCE TO LEARN SOCIAL SKILLS

The remembrance group learned strategies to remember word lists and main ideas and specific details in the stories. The reasoning group focused on identifying patterns and using this information to solve problems. These capabilities are useful for completing order forms and reading schedules. The processing speed group practiced localization and identification of visual information related to searching for telephone numbers, reading instructions in the recipes, and responding to traffic signs and signals. One might conclude that the training, for example, focuses on certain types of cognition memory, argumentation, and concentration: it can improve the efficiency, even as we get older, but it does not make us much more effective. One reason for these mixed results may be that the specific training types selected emphasize the tasks that are performed primarily by the frontal lobes of the brain. It is also the first part of the brain that shuts off and deteriorates due to the physical and / or emotional stress caused by the demands of modern life. When he opened the eye of the mind, as pictures and language teach us to see, he said, "Just because pictures tend to be little used, they are less common, less automatic and therefore possibly more flexible." The underused part of the brain referred to is the parietal lobes, in which the sensory inputs are integrated, analogies are constructed, eye-hand coordination is coordinated, and attention is focused. Although attention is under the control of the frontal lobes and is the key to learning and remembering, the parietal lobes play a central role in attention control, control of the gaze, and integration of the components of the seen. In conjunction with the temporal lobes, they are reminiscent of strings of numbers as well as visual and non-verbal memories.

The parietal lobes are extremely active in preschool children who think more visually than verbally. Formal education with a focus on reading and writing is changing the focus of language development. Unfortunately, this also slows down the learning process and creative thinking. Studies show that combining words and images in our minds improves memory and understanding. In addition, visual memories survive more with age than voice-based memories. This may be partly due to the fact that brain activity in the frontal lobes drops when attention is divided, as is the case when humans perform multiple tasks. Of course, some people retain strong visual skills during their school years. Many of them become artists, architects or engineers. People who rely heavily on verbalization are more likely to have careers in law, administration or journalism. The good news is that visualization can be improved with practice at any age.

In addition to visual and spatial memory, the hippocampus plays an important role in regulating the body's response to life-threatening emergencies. Chronic stress can lead to loss of hippocampal neurons and atrophy of dendrites that bind to other brain cells. Some of the post-traumatic stress disorders of war veterans, such as memory weakness, are related to a reduced hippocampus. However, it has also been discovered that new brain cells can be produced in the hippocampus even in adults. Brain research revealed that both age groups, when asked to remember word lists, used the left frontal lobe, but younger people also used the hippocampus, which was associated with wordless memories.

Brain scans indicate that people use different parts of their brain when performing different types of math. Our left frontal lobe "lights up" when we perform accurate calculations, but our left and right parietal lobes are activated when we make estimates and count on our fingers. In addition, people who have difficulty with numbers, a disease known as "dyscalculia," also have problems in designing time and direction. They are usually chronically retarded, easily disoriented in new environments, making decisions based more on intuition rather than logic, having difficulty in planning activities, and keeping track of the money. It's not about intelligence or memory. People with dyscalculia can be highly articulated and excellent authors and readers. The problem is the functional integration of the brain.

Improvement of memory is only the tip of the iceberg in terms of the learning capacity of the adult brain. With a little practice, the average person can memorize extensive lists of words and numbers that are of little practical value to impress friends at parties. To be truly effective, memory must be connected with meaning and purpose. The mental training of visualization is critical to developing the ability to productively use the information we remember. Because the modern world demands more from us, we should not settle for less than optimal use of our brains.

What we hear and interpret is a function of limited hearing and vision and the limitations of processing this information, which is based on previous experiences in our brain. Feel that it is the truth and explain that it is unrealistic and arrogant. It is deceptive. That's why we should and if we do; declare humbly as "our impressions" and do not confirm that it is the absolute truth. Understanding this scheme gives you the knowledge of the [intellectual] perception error that leads to stress and its correction. Intellectual health manifests itself in a globally beneficial perspective, policies, plans and actions in their field that would flourish not only for patients but for all those involved in medical care. Direct or indirect!

EMOTIONAL HEALTH

Everyone knows the different positive and negative emotions. It is very easy to say that we have to overcome fear, anger, hate, depression, jealousy, and so on. It is also very easy to work for positive emotions such as peace, happiness, love and so on. But the important difficulty is how to do it. The human brain itself is such that those parts involved in the emotions are hardly under the control of the instrumental parts of the thought! Moreover, there is no clarity about parts of the brain that are related to spiritual growth. Therefore, most emotions do not always follow the example of spiritual and intellectual processes, although spiritual health and intellectual health can essentially avoid many emotional disturbances. They have good autonomy and volatility. Therefore, additional specific measures must be taken to promote emotional health. We must understand here that emotional health depends to a great extent on the strength of our limbic system and the autonomic nervous system, although it is to a certain extent influenced by central and hormonal nerve activities.

At first it may be difficult, but after a few days of exercise you will feel comfortable. But you can find out for yourself whether you are losing weight, feeling energetic, optimistic, feeling younger or not. Also find out if you have stopped beating in small adversities or imaginary fears. Check if unwanted sweating stops or not. Find out if your lipid or blood sugar profile is useful. Emotional health clearly has a positive effect on your physical and instinctive health. This can be called a by-product of emotional health!

The meaning of BHASTRIKA is bellows. You should breathe deeply and exhale by imitating the effect of the bellows. The rhythm of the bellows is necessary, but it is important to avoid the pulling. UJJAYI means victory. Breathe out slowly, hard and completely. Now pull the larynx, ie the region of the voice box, partially together and breathe with a high-intensity sound. There are no precautions and restrictions for UJJAYI, except for respiratory injury.

We must pay attention to our instinctive and physical health to overcome unpleasant sensations and resulting emotional disturbances. Only a few simple tips that you can add many more to your experience can contribute to your emotional health, though most are not essential. You need to sleep well, otherwise you will become more irritated. Get enough rest, because another tiredness depresses you, pulls you back and makes you negative.

Instinctive health- The mental, intellectual and emotional health forms the basis for the instinctive health. But you can also benefit more from the following relief measures! From a biological point of view, we humans also inherit the instincts found in mammals and birds. These instincts are an integral part of life and are largely related to the release hormones as well as metabolic activities. Therefore, if the instincts are not satisfied, the stress generated is enormous and much more dangerous than mere emotional stress and must therefore be overcome by "instinctive stress" to gain instinctive health.

What we hear and interpret is a function of limited hearing and vision and the limitations of processing this information, which is based on previous experiences in our brain. Feel that it is the truth and explain that it is unrealistic and arrogant. It is deceptive. That's why we should and if we do; declare humbly as "our impressions" and do not confirm that it is the absolute truth. Understanding this scheme gives you the knowledge of the [intellectual] perception error that leads to stress and its correction. Intellectual health manifests itself in a globally beneficial perspective, policies, plans and actions in their field that would flourish not only for patients but for all those involved in medical care. Direct or indirect!

Emotional Health We all know the different positive and negative emotions. It is very easy to say that we have to overcome fear, anger, hate, depression, jealousy, and so on. It is also very easy to work for positive emotions such as peace, happiness, love and so on. But the important difficulty is how to do it. The human brain itself is such that those parts involved in the emotions are hardly under the control of the instrumental parts of the thought! Moreover, there is no clarity about parts of the brain that are related to spiritual growth. Therefore, most emotions do not always follow the example of spiritual and intellectual processes, although spiritual health and intellectual health can essentially avoid many emotional disturbances. They have good autonomy and volatility. Therefore, additional specific measures must be taken to promote emotional health.

We must understand here that emotional health depends to a great extent on the strength of our limbic system and the autonomic nervous system, although it is to a certain extent influenced by central and hormonal nerve activities. What practical relevance do these facts have? The relevance is that we can practice following Pranayama's to tighten those parts and achieve a high level of emotional health!

So, what are we looking for in our "leaders"? Let us develop a list of criteria that influence our perceptions, who the leader is and what defines them. As we seek leaders with greater balance, agility and patience to minimize the impact of the uncertainty of the situation, here are some key features that are critical to good leaders. Our initial perception of the serenity of a good leader is reflected in his attitude, body language and general presentation, but we go further. Maintains honesty and is not emotional. Stick to proven behaviors and make informed decisions as needed. You cannot perceive that you have your feelings up your sleeve. Emotions are controlled by your subconscious and manifest when you least expect them when they are not controlled. Emotions are deep anchors that are created and evolve as we develop in life through what we have learned at the beginning of life. If it is not controlled, the people who go will go with the idea that you are not objective enough and seem too passionate about the situation in question.

Good leaders retain their composure and can express concern and care. It can delegate. It is important that leaders understand this rationale. One alone cannot take responsibility for doing all things and using others to participate in the process. By assigning parts of the common task to specific persons, they rewards them with the responsibility of being part of the team and their adaptation in the process. A good leader understands this and involves the team in all aspects of the goal. This gives all participants a sense of belonging in the final evaluation and drives them more and more to their destination.

A good leader is a great communicator. Good leaders understand their choice of words, the tone and clarity of their voices, and the body communication signals presented in the presentation contribute to how well the group has understood the given task and where it fits with the overall image. If these skills are not part of the overall composition of the responsible person, they should take the initiative to work in this key area of leadership. If you have most of the qualities associated with good leaders, and this is a skill that requires work, then leave a big gap in the team's response to your leadership. Show confidence Trust is exemplified by both external and internal behavior. It is easy to recognize and accept as a trait that most people want because it shows a person who can handle the job, position and orientation that seems to follow him.

Really safe people are calm and modest. You already know what they think. You want to know what you think. Safe people are accepted to ascend and generally end up at higher professional levels. They left no obstacles along the way and found roads around them. You will see them as group, team and business leaders, since people naturally want to follow a strong and self-confident personality. Safe people do not need excellence, they know what they have achieved, and this is represented as a positive internal feeling and strong and positive body communication. You don't need the validation of others - because the validation is based on the person and depends on the background and life experience in your life. Show positive attitude, your attitude is directly reflected in the disposition of your subconscious mind. We all begin to create a level playing field, but at the age of three to four, we develop our internal moral compass and a set of values that determine our adult behavior later in life. A child who is constantly praised has developed a positive attitude, while a child who constantly listens to how stupid and stupid he is, on the contrary, tends to think negatively and, ultimately, to self-sabotage in his life.

Followers of a leader are always attentive to the actions, behavior, relationships and general behavior of their leader. Use all situations to demonstrate your experience and leadership determination. Good quality leaders set the tone for your organization. A positive attitude neutralizes chaos and allows a good leader to adjust his course through negativity. The followers of a leader feed on the positive attitude in times of uncertainty. Maintain a positive attitude and move on.

Good leaders retain their serenity and never show signs of doubt. They respond resolutely. Their communication is conviction, trust and authority. Its nature of transmission gives its followers a sense of calm when everything is under control. If doubts arise with the followers, chaos can arise. Followers want a leader to lead their movement forward, be it a small group or a large company. A good leader understands this principle and does not hesitate to convey the message. We have already reported on good communication and where it fits in with the delivery of the message. When situations justify a change, the followers want to know details and appreciate a leader who acts resolutely on their behalf.

To take responsibility. If a leader is responsible for the organization they already made the decision to take responsibility and take the necessary action to resolve the problem. In reality, executives are better off in crisis and change phases when they are fully committed to solving the challenge. Accountability denies the negative thinking that can quickly penetrate the team and its goal. A good leader accepts their responsibility and responsibility are the sum total of the entire team, and has delegated that sense of importance to the team members and their share of responsibility. It has the ability to inspire others. Inspiration and motivation are two completely different values. Motivation is an internal describtion driven by the inspiration of others. An inappropriate name is the term motivational speaker. In reality, they should be referred to as inspirational speakers because nobody can motivate the individual as himself. A personal improvement seminar will definitely inspire us to leave the function and motivate us to meet the seminar standards. This change is created by creating in the person a sense of urgency that motivates them to begin the new behavior. Unfortunately, most people give up at the beginning of the process without noticing that it takes at least twenty-one times for the new behavior to be challenged to bring about lasting change.

Act as if they knew what they are doing. Good leaders know that one of the most effective ways to keep calm in difficult times is to act as if you've gone through the process before. Leaders who demonstrate the ability to solve the problem with their initiative and determined action have a strong leadership presence that gives their followers confidence. The crisis and change can cause concern, which can often be expressed in concern and doubt. Doubt can also create fear that is destructive to any challenging situation. By maintaining a balance, the best leaders remain cold, calm and laid back. This basic behavior allows them to create a macro and evaluate the overall picture before making important decisions to control the situation. Serenity calms the supporters of the leader and creates a safe working environment. The human mind is a beautiful creation: powerful, agile and adaptable; unfortunately, is just as susceptible to anxiety, restlessness and endless wanderings as he is capable of being great. In life and death we sometimes have no time for these endless rambles or for the fear itself;

instead, these are moments of pure intuition, of instinct, of enabling our inner knowing to gain the upper hand.

Regardless of whether we are looking for a creative solution to reinvent our workplace, we only have to make an important decision with our internal compass and wonder what the best step is.

Achieving our soul and voice can be both complicated. Stress, demands, ambitions and indulgences of the contemporary lifestyle, our mind is full of incessant ideas and conversations. Learning to silence your mind and channeling your inner dialogue with you, and learning to control it, is therefore both an art and a central survival instinct. The most popular recipe for modulating and tempering the human mind is meditation, and rightly so. Meditation in its various forms and formats has enabled us over the centuries to develop new ideas, perspectives and discoveries, and to help anchor the eternal and the eternal. In various traditions, schools of thought and wisdom systems, meditation has helped, and helped so many hearts and minds. Even today, many meditation methods and techniques are as relevant as they were when they were first articulated in the annals of time and history. However, the central intentions and concepts of meditation often differ drastically from the rest of our lifestyle. Therefore, it is a secret that often escapes us along with its gifts. The result: Silencing our minds seems to be an even more discouraging business. How is the mind silenced? How do you meditate on submission? The answer is simple: for your mind to give you, you must first learn to surrender.

In fact, as we begin to pounder, we send commands to our mind and body to conform and change the meditative way we want to experience. I have seen one meditation student meditate after another. Meditation is a state and not an action, and therefore we need to fully intervene to fully experience it: mind, body and soul. We need to get out of our internal and external dialogues to experience, accept, and exalt this space into which the silence penetrates. The key is the delivery. Indulge in the experiences you have in your meditation practice as you learn to constantly master your mind. Allow your soul to guide you on the right path instead of finding your way to your destination. This may even mean that you do not want to meditate for a long time, are increasingly aware of how chatty your mind really is, and even inspire you to change your habits and meditation routines. As long as you are disciplined and patient, you will continue to seek to control your mind, even if you do not spend hours each week in peace and quiet. Remember, the idea is to make allies with your mind to earn it; Do not crush or eliminate. The time or journey you need is very personal and sacred. Do not try to accelerate it; Give up instead.

Adults learn through experience. We learn behavior through experience. This is the fact of the flagpole of the educational world. This flag is visible to all, and here educators know if they are training hard or soft skills.. "While conceptual learning is important, the most important one makes a leap forward. The question is, "What transformation do you want?" What final condition do you envision for your organization, and what behavioral adjustment does your employee need to make before this vision can be realized? The answer to this question often goes through the corporate culture. employees who value agility and responsiveness. Properly conducted experimental training can create fertile conditions for rapid adaptation to corporate culture, regardless of the direction you choose to take. Whether it's agility and responsiveness, sustainability or lean systems, it can be achieved. However, to receive the greatest rewards, you must make two commitments.

First, you must adopt the experimental training model for its ability to quickly influence behavior. Second, because everyone plays a role in corporate culture, you must commit to training almost anyone. Recognize that this is a huge distance for most companies. You'll find that there are many powerful experiential training capabilities that can help you improve your business's performance without seriously affecting your corporate culture. All significant effects on your leadership core should be considered. However, if you are looking for this comprehensive modification, you must plan the results and deploy resources. Bring along a ladder high enough to reach at least the lowest branches.

If you do not have leadership, you lose the ability to take full advantage of the new culture that makes this training possible. You can use your entire training time and effort on sustainability or agility, and your business will be very smart in these areas. You can use experiential training to make the lessons real, but if you do not have an expansive, dedicated, and sustained leadership, you will fail.

One of the key benefits of a comprehensive immersion campaign is that it not only controls your corporate culture, but also enhances every aspect of your ability to succeed by creating a predominant leadership culture. Fortunately, the guiding principles are almost universal. The same principles used to successfully lead a project team are also used to manage a sales organization or technical staff. The better these principles are integrated into the operational habits of your employees, the more benefits you have.

Immersion training allows each participant to participate fully in each step, be it a leader or a follower. It allows the immediate clarification of the relationship between actions and consequences. It offers the opportunity to learn to make things better through polite analysis and experimentation. You can experience the consequences of errors in a training environment and not in an office environment where they would be much more expensive. Compress the learning cycle when working from months and years to several days. It is an experience that helps to internalize positive practices of teamwork, leadership, communication and the variables you choose.

Start and finish right: At the beginning and end of this visceral, emotional experience they are important instruction and analysis elements. The format of the experience is of the utmost importance, but to avoid spills at the end, class time is very easy. Make them feel the stress of having eyes and expectations and learning what it means to make a decision and defend it. Everyone can work in a team and learn to rely on each other to achieve a goal.

THE POWER OF RAPID REPETITION

BEHAVIOURAL CHANGE

The reduction in time for behavior change is due to the fact that the same leadership patterns as in the workplace are imitated in training, only that they are fast and clear. In the unguided and unanalyzed workplace, decisions are made. However, the consequences of these decisions are days or months in the future and are rarely fully understood. Of course, the aspects of interpersonal communication of impressions, perceptions and clarity are never addressed. Compress this pattern and repeat it several times in a few days in a guided environment, where the connection between decision and consequence is clear and behavior changes quickly. Once you have ridden a bicycle, it would be good to stop there and slap your back, but there is always more to do in the practice of immersion. The overlap is achieved by immediately moving on to another round of introduction, experience, analysis and bridge then another, then another, etc. This training will guide the leaders; Make mistakes, evaluate decisions and repeat them in rapid succession. Entrepreneur magazine illustrates how immersion training can inspire people. "Many participate in leadership training and believe that their most valuable lessons will be in the area of policies and procedures, but they will gain more fundamental knowledge that will ultimately be more valuable." The article goes on to say that "the owners who valued their experiences best were those who distanced themselves most from them."

Those who are more distant and have no external distractions have the greatest opportunity to have a clear idea of what teaching and experience mean to them. You have time to think, not only during the analysis and bridge phase, but also during the downtime. It is this hidden time outside business hours that can include the principles and values in a person's decision cycle. Facilitating the learning of the desired message in the clearest and deepest way possible is the beginning of the future, and it is another product of experimental training that cannot compete with less involved methods.

One of the reasons why soft skills progress so little, despite the mountains of writing, speaking and training, is that teachers write on a panel full of student education. The falsification of writing with a large chalk in the small open spaces of the board or in large letters on top of the existing writing even obstructs the understanding of the planned lessons. If a proper understanding is never achieved, the perseverance required to take a lesson and create a habit cannot begin. The difficulty of implementing new behaviors is exacerbated by the fact that the work environment in which these behaviors are supposed to work is not a guided experience. There are many activities that are not suitable for 8-1 / 2 x 11 edges. When we get to the point where we want to apply, we see mutated lessons adapted by a person in a job where the cause and effect of the guide are seldom obvious. The results are mutated and misallocated if they are even recognized. This approach makes everyone shrug in frustration.

Some would rightly say that it is a person's background, education and professional experience that allows him to quickly learn new materials. They are able to combine new information with existing experience to create new knowledge. This is completely correct and extremely valid in a difficult skill. The problem found in the soft skills environment is that the existing managerial experience, if any, is trial and error and is rarely anchored in precise guiding principles. Your experience will be the confusing scribble on the board. The way to overcome the conditions of laundering of the student's education is to find a clean slate. It must have a place where a clear message can be delivered and a method that changes the behavior beyond the last slide. With the immersion method, you get a clean board for almost all employees of your company. Write in the upper left corner of the board Guided leadership experience. Write "Real Leadership Experience." For more efficient progress, these two factors must fit. Actual experience is often referred to as work experience, whose overweight is not controlled. Guided experience is call professional development. Broadening my definition of experiential training goes beyond books, speeches and seminars, to a level where a person makes leadership decisions that have consequences.

Follow-up after training: constant reinforcement of the knowledge acquired through complementary teaching material, interaction in the chain of command and advanced and guided training. Guided leadership experiences are almost non-existent. To be fair, most major business schools have included experience training and role play in their curriculum. Fortunately, the guided nature of the experience does not provide a basis for the actual experience on which it can be built.

Write your message on the clean board of leadership experience and continue to develop your company's leadership. Immersion training is the best way to convey a clear message that quickly changes people's behavior. The relatively dramatic nature of training also prepares people to absorb new information that can transform their corporate culture, no matter what they want. As people evolved in their primitive world, the need for survival became a fundamental response to life-threatening situations. These two reactions, called flight or fight, had a dramatic impact on human development and development. The mentality was very basic at that time because survival was critical. Confrontation situations with other people and animals often caused anxiety. As the level of anxiety increased, the need to reduce it was also critical at this point. Some people developed a stronger and more aggressive response to anxiety called response struggle, while others developed agility, speed and increased use of the senses: smell, sight and hearing, called response (flight) era. If you evaluated the primitive residents who did not develop these two reactions, you would have to agree that these first humans are probably extinct. The key to understanding this information is that when people developed the basic responses to escape or fight against the environment, they also learned to think a little more and more, depending on how they responded to any of the mechanisms. This information learned would eventually develop greater awareness or awareness. The human with his greatest understanding realized that he did not have to respond to every impulse that was presented to him and began to develop conscious control. He gradually drove the bottom

Your subconscious mind has evolved since birth and is the sum of all the experiences made through the senses and emotional values you make through the experiences of life. In other words, it is like a file system with all the different experiences you have had in your life. Imagine your subconscious as a space for information files. A room full of files, some thin files, others thick, depending on the experience of life in a particular area. These files are sometimes positive. When they praised you when you were a child, or vice versa, when you received degrading or derogatory statements about your commitment to the world around you. We all remember many positive situations in our lives and the moments when we left the situation and we felt bad at that particular moment. Some of us have always been praised for having a good performance in school, working well with classmates, completing their projects on time, having a good attitude in school or in the social environment. These are examples of positive files that continue to increase in thickness as we move forward with more file additions. The more positive the file space, the stronger the tendency to react positively to life situations. Furthermore, it is a tendency to react negatively to persistent negative shipments when children because the fundamental files have been structured in this way. Remember that the subconscious has no justification only accept information. This information may work to your advantage or disadvantage. Although you are consciously in control of your daily decisions, this is constantly influenced by the subconscious information space that is your true self.

Consciousness has the ability to think and rationalize which decision will be the best at this time, but cannot implement that real decision until the subconscious mind agrees and can focus its energies on the goal. Remember that the subconscious mind represents 88 percent of the total capacity and definitely cancels the decision-making process when your files related to this particular situation are very extensive by experience.

Self-management: self-confidence leads to self-management. Self-administration is about controlling your emotions and actions. They control themselves from impulsive behaviors. They develop openness, adaptability, performance and optimism. How do you react to certain situations? Do you react to people and situations? There are small differences between these two words, but in practice there is a big difference in meaning. The reaction play an important role in equalization. For example, if you have to wait on a busy day in a long line while traffic moves very slowly, will it get impatient? Are you yelling at other drivers and honking or waiting patiently for traffic to clear. When you are impatient, you respond emotionally to traffic. When you react, you tend to lose your reason. On the other hand, if the other person shows patience, not responding and, therefore, is more understanding and thoughtful. After all, traffic must continue at some point! Self-management is synonymous with adaptability, transparency, performance and optimism.

Social awareness: your self-esteem and self-management take you to the next step of social awareness. They are open to understanding the needs, emotions and concerns of others. They can pick up emotional cues, feel socially relaxed and recognize the power play in a group or organization. To develop your EQ, you need to see and feel others in your shoes. People with excellent social awareness should be more service oriented, empathic and organizational. These are the main characteristics of social consciousness. Social awareness at its best provides a natural response to people, taking into account their situation and needs as much as possible. If you have these characteristics, your EQ can be considered high.

Relationship management: the last area you need to develop to improve your EQ is relationship management. We can see this trait in relation to their profession. This is the aspect of your EQ that allows you to inspire other people and help them reach their full potential. It is also important to negotiate successfully, resolve conflicts and work towards a common goal with others. Its success in the latter area is directly related to its success in the other three areas, since the administration consists in interacting successfully with other people. In short, efficient management is not just about doing the job.

Emotional intelligence can be divided into five main categories that each individual tries to master.

Self-knowledge: Before a person can read another person's emotions, they should be able to read their own. Self-awareness requires that an individual is aware of and able to deal with their own emotions. For example, a self-conscious person who fidgets, realizes that he is nervous, and takes steps to calm himself. This self-confidence also includes self-esteem, which is always helpful when negotiating your way through interpersonal communication.

Self-regulation: While no one has complete control over the emotions that he experiences, some can control how long those emotions last. Self-regulation is the ability to relieve negative emotions such as anger or anxiety. The individual can take a breath and look at his situation in a more positive light. People who control self-regulation are able to control negative impulses, have personal integrity standards, take responsibility for their actions and are able to adapt to new situations.

Motivation: An emotionally intelligent person has personal goals and can recognize that others also have their own goals. To achieve one of these goals, a person needs to be motivated to improve, to seize opportunities and to be optimistic. A person with a high level of emotional intelligence will be able to reconcile their own goals with the goals of organizations in which they are involved. This can include the workplace, the volunteer organization, and even circles of friends.

Empathy: This is the ability to recognize the feelings or motivations behind the signals of another person. This also determines which signals you need to send in return. Sensitive people can anticipate the needs of others, empower their employees, read the emotional state of a person or group, and understand the dynamics of power in relationships or groups.

Social Skills: A well-developed set of interpersonal skills is critical to success in both personal relationships and careers. People with good social skills are able to convince others, send clear messages, manage others, manage change, settle disagreements, and build connections with others.

Of course, not everyone will have a naturally high EQ. However, the aspects and skills that make up high emotional intelligence can be learned. Everyone can learn to recognize their emotions, to regulate them and to react appropriately in the group dynamics. The process often requires not only interaction with others, but also self-reflection. Of course, as you learn to read yourself and control your own negative emotions, you will be better at reading the people around you, responding to their signals, and navigating the waters of every social situation!

Technology has influence our means of communication. It is often evident when students and instructors interact in the classroom. Instead of relying upon technological devices and social networking websites, they are required to develop one-on-one interpersonal relationships that are highly productive. One of the highly important elements needed for the development of effective classroom interactions is a well-developed emotional intelligence.

Emotional Intelligence (EQ) is an art that must be developed in these times to intelligently address your emotions in any situation in life. This ability paves the way for success and complacency in every area of your life.

You may think that emotional intelligence cannot be taught, but you would be wrong. The best thing about EQ is that it can be developed and the more you practice it, the better you will be. Social work and care are relationships based occupations. Regardless of whether we work with service users, other industry professionals or colleagues between agencies, relationships are the focus of our activities. When you develop emotional intelligence, you must first start with yourself. Take a step back and see how you react to people. Do you judge people too fast? The stereotypes of them? Make decisions without knowing all the facts? Be honest we all do it at some point, but when you develop EQ, you must take its place. Be open and accept your views and perspectives. Just one or two more seconds to consider all the factors is a great way to start your trip. Remember to separate emotions from "reason." Social workers and caregivers can easily confuse the two. EQ helps distinguish between the use of your emotions and mere feeling. In our profession it is not easy to separate emotions, meanings, perceptions and actions from each other. We learn to rely on the wisdom of our emotions to guide us. This is essentially emotional intelligence. It would be a great euphemism to say that working in the social and nursing profession is not stressful. We regularly face emotional situations, often highly charged. This is a point where EQ can really help us with development. Start over with yourself on how to deal with stressful situations?

The last way to develop your emotional intelligence is the simplest, but also that most people overlook. Take the time to recognize that you are practicing EQ and that you are doing well in the daily challenges we all face. Give yourself some recognition. Only you are responsible for your feelings. So, if you have a moment, congratulate yourself on what you have accomplished. They definitely deserve it, and even if they don't thank you, everyone around you would agree, so keep it up.

Most people recognize that social skills are necessary to succeed, both personally and professionally. Think of the successful people you know, who are generally self-confident, know how to effectively interact with themselves and how they understand and work effectively with others. Social skills are needed to succeed in friendships, school life, community life and, ultimately, working life.

Numerous studies have shown that the success of a career depends more on the emotional intelligence of the individual than on the technical or intellectual skills. In particular, Emotional intelligence can be improved and developed through lifelong learning. Emotional intelligence refers to four areas: self-esteem (for example, knowing your strengths and weaknesses), self-management (for example, knowing how to motivate yourself), awareness of others (for example, empathy or the ability to "read" accurately other people's facial expressions) and social delicacy (for example, knowing how to influence others).

But how can our wards have an idea of when they have fewer opportunities than their parents to learn social and emotional intelligence through spontaneous and unstructured play and communication with their peers? Due to the climate of anxiety and increased safety precautions, children have little time to play, walk, explore and learn from other neglected experiences with other children. They do not have the degree of freedom that children of previous generations had to play in groups to assume roles as leaders or followers, express their opinions, learn to communicate and influence others, and their own strengths and weaknesses through daily experiences . To understand with your classmates.

How do we deal as parents with this tendency to decrease social skills? How can we educate our ward on the social skills they need to prepare for life? Here are 10 tips to get started.

1. To help your child develop social skills, you need to find time to be social and communicate with your children. Dining with your family is a perfect opportunity. By sitting down to eat at the table, family members have the opportunity to share, laugh and joke about their experiences of the day, or to support and comfort each other. These daily interactions help children develop their listening, alternation and expression skills. I recommend that you make sure that the television is turned off during dinner and that the children learn to sit at the table until everyone has finished eating or talking. Having dinner together is also an ideal way to teach your child to behave. For example, the proper use of cutlery or ask to leave the table.

2. Children learn from what they see, what they do, not what they say they should do. Be a model of your child's social skills. Take every opportunity, for example, to show how much you try to understand others. You can do this by demonstrating how you think about other people's feelings, how you are trying to "follow in their footsteps" to better understand what the world looks like from your perspective, how to think carefully about how you do it. Try saying something to someone and anticipate how to "listen" first, before saying it.

3. Explain to your child how and why they need to demonstrates these skills. Ask them how they could do better.

4. If your child mentions a disagreement with another child, take the time to discuss it together. Take the "page" of the other child and help him understand the different perspectives and the possible reasons why the other child acted that way. Encourage your child to tell you what the other child wants to say and talk to him about how he would feel if he had heard that. Whenever your ward is ready, assist him or her to discuss the matter with the other child and solve it for himself.

5. When you talk to your child and explain the choices you have made in life, there are many ways to communicate social and emotional intelligence. If you face a difficult decision or a painful experience, do not hide it and do not try to "protect" your child. Be open and speak

with your child in a language he can understand. Communicate your thoughts and feelings and ask for their thoughts and feelings. Explore with them how they handled the situation or what choices they made. The ability to speak in a "language" of emotions is an integral part of emotional intelligence.

6. When your child shows his feelings, whether angry or happy, pay attention to his feelings and discuss his son. Be a role model for someone who reads the feelings of others and reacts sensitively. If they are injured, ask them kind and sensitive questions to investigate the damage and discover the best way to improve it. If you are happy, explore and enjoy happiness, ask what has made it so good for you and your child to learn to experience that happiness again in the future.

7. Traditional board games are a great way to teach children social skills. Buy or dust out games such as drafts, dominoes, quads and card games that are fun, inspiring, and conducive to concentration and strengthen communication and social interaction skills. Learning to Play is a creation of Mind Lab, an out-of-school educational program that teaches the thinking and social skills of children playing board games around the world.

8. Explain that to enjoy playing, we all have to comply with the rules, respect our partners and respect the outcome of the game. Whether we win or lose to have fun together, we can't be happy to win and we can't get angry if we lose. When we play many games together, there are many opportunities for each of us to win and sometimes lose. Either way, we had fun playing together.

9. When your child wins or loses, at the end of the game, summarize what he learned from the game and then ask him: "What did you learn from this game?" "What could you do differently next time?"

10. Praise your child a lot if he does well. Either to understand the needs of a friend, communicate their own feelings in a calm way that allows one to discuss it, or to do their time to do their homework

before playing let them know what made them good and successful of what they are proud of. In contrast to punishment and reproach, children learn much more effectively from praise and recognition.

These ideas and tips are just a starting point. Try to encouraged yourself to look for daily opportunities to develop your child's social skills and emotional intelligence by taking advantage of situations spontaneously and taking time to do your best. Not only do you give your child the skills that will make it effective, but they also imagine that the time you spend with your child is of a much higher quality, and you will find that you are getting closer and closer and enjoying yourself more than ever. appreciating each other more than ever before.

HOW TO KNOW HOW EFFECTIVE YOUR SOCIAL

Emotional intelligence is, in the classical sense, a person's ability to treat and regulate their emotions, as well as other people's emotions. Of course, the second is more difficult, but not impossible, depending on the approach used.

Emotional intelligence measures a person's ability to predict emotional response in a given situation. It is a developed skill that is worthwhile because it assists you, the business owner (or even an experienced higher who works for someone else) to maintain the advantage over the situation. If you can predict the emotional response of the other person, you can distort the outcome of the situation. You may consider this manipulative, but it is not manipulative in a negative sense. It basically means that you are sensitive enough to understand what the other person wants and needs before that person knows what those things are. Being a sensitive person is something very positive and should not be confused with hypersensitivity. It means that you have the ability to put the other person's wishes, needs and feelings in front of yours, which in turn means that you can solve the other person's problems relatively quickly and quite successfully. Because he is emotionally intelligent (sensitive), he probably has calm behavior that has a positive effect on the other person. When emotions do not cloud thoughts, real progress can be made in the situation. It also means that they can lead the situation and achieve a lot together. The bottom line is that people only buy products and / or services from other people with whom they can connect emotionally.

How to know if your social media marketing strategy is effective? If you really have the urge to succeed while using social media marketing as one of your main tools, you must first make sure that your social media marketing strategy is strong and you can really trust it. Take your business to the next level. The amount of your emotional intelligence plays an important role in your strategy. Some key factors to consider when implementing your social media marketing strategy. Tell a really good story: Although social networks are a very important part of your social media marketing strategy, it is very important that you remember that it is not your entire strategy. Of course, it has great potential to help you succeed. One of the main purposes of his presence in social networks is to effectively communicate his story with other people. Of course, your story must be very well written and interesting. However, you must also touch your readers on an emotional / human level.

Your story (at least to some extent) should also be the story of your readers. If the other person can relate to what you are writing, you probably want to deepen your relationship and interact directly and frequently with you. If you can show your readers (through your story) that you understand what they are going through or what you went through because you were there yourself, you will make them eat from your palm! You will be curious to know what to offer next. Practice your listening comprehension: One of the most common (and most serious) problems is that people don't listen to what the other person says and what they want and need.

Once you have heard what the other person has said, it is your turn to speak. Your patience will definitely be worth it. When you have good listening skills (and practice these skills), you not only learn what the other person wants and needs, but also learn all kinds of other things from the other person. That's fair. Hopes and this is one of our main goals for the other person to listen and benefit from our experience. Why is it so ridiculous that the other person expect the same from you? It is important that you remember that it must be a dialogue and not a monologue. You should never do it to listen to yourself. It is a valuable exchange of ideas (or at least it should be).

Make your mission to help the other person in every possible way: social networks are incredible, because the opportunities offered to your business are almost unlimited. Every time you interact with one of your online connections, you are helping that person in some way. The good you have done may not be immediately apparent, but it will eventually be obvious to you and the other person. This is the basis of building and maintaining relationships. In the spirit of "one hand washes the other," if you help the other person, they will return the favor and somehow help you.

Social skills

Managers need to know how to resolve conflicts between their team members, customers or suppliers. Learning conflict resolution skills is crucial if you want to succeed. Develop your communication skills. Correct communication is crucial for good leadership. You must learn to improve those skills. As a leader, you can easily improve your team's loyalty by praising when you win.

In business and personal development, different themes, themes and theories become fashionable and are going out of style. Many people look for the latest theory and expect it to offer a magical solution. Maybe it could be, but again it couldn't be. Often, the well experiences can assist with the answers if they are understood and used correctly. I want to investigate whether there is a connection between personal resilience and emotional intelligence (given an established concept) and whether the development of one or the other, or both, offers benefits. Why it matters. The current economic situation in many parts of the world is a challenge for both organizations and individuals. Organizations need capable and strong leaders at all levels. People need to be able to cope with the pressures of these difficult times and maintain their ability to succeed at work and live a balanced and productive life. I will show you an overview of emotional intelligence and the role it plays in quality leadership training and good interpersonal skills. I will address the 6 components of personal resilience that help people overcome difficult times. From there, I will explore how one's development can support and help each other. What happens when people start to improve one of them? You will discover that you can help the organization and people in many different areas improve performance and morale.

The emotionally intelligent person would normally show the following:

Ability to motivate oneself to reach certain goals. The ability to persevere despite adverse frustration, things that go wrong. Ability to control impulses and delay satisfaction, d. H. Move instant enjoyment to achieve a long-term goal, for example. Financial security. Mental resistance, which is characterized by the ability to regulate one's mood and prevents the ability to think through stress is affected. Ability to show empathy, be sensitive to the feelings or emotions of others. Ability to continue with other people. Ability to enter "flow" or "the zone". Emotional intelligence can be taught. There is a general agreement that, unlike an IQ, which can hardly be changed through education, the most important emotional competences can be learned and improved, if taught, especially since childhood.

Emotional self-regulation - This is the ability to go back before, during or after an emotionally charged situation, or press the Pause button which frees us from prisoners of our feelings

Emotional self-motivation - Self-motivated people not only know what they feel, but they can turn their anxiety or negative emotions into positive and productive emotions and actions. They can evoke feelings of trust, optimism and enthusiasm.

Empathy - Once a basis is established for the first three competencies (all intrapersonal), EI begins to influence a person's interactions with others. Empathy may seem inappropriate or unnecessary from a traditional business perspective. In today's economy, where teamwork, intercultural sensitivity, training and mentoring are essential, empathy is a fundamental skill.

Relationship management (social skills) - This competition combines sincere care and kindness with a purpose. To effectively manage relationships, leaders must understand and channel their emotions in a useful way, be motivated to take positive action and empathize with others. Instead of trying to manage or manipulate relationships, it is about defining a positive tone for collaboration, regardless of circumstances. It can help all parties to find common ground in which collaboration can lead to movement in the desired direction.

What emotional intelligence is NOT

However, there is a problem with the way some people quickly get used to the argument that academic skills / IQ are not a guarantee of success in life. They say out loud "with others" as a critical skill / emotional competence that is essential for social success. Although we recognize that "interpersonal skills" are in fact an essential skill, my observations of some of those who emphasize that "understanding with others" to succeed concern me that this must be done at all costs, In other words, INTEGRITY and SINCERITY of purpose / intention are NOT considered. The greatest danger associated with this type of thinking is that, without realizing it, it gives a false credibility to false and manipulative individuals who use their social relationships for selfish purposes. (For example, to look good or get broad approval from anyone who considers them important or relevant). For this reason, it seems important to uniquely identify certain cases in which "being together with others" does not lead to emotional intelligence in the TRUE sense of the term. Anyone who loses sight of the fact that EMOTIONAL INTEGRITY is more important and essential than obtaining social recognition is having long-term difficulties. To stay true to oneself and NOT be a social chameleon or have emotional integrity, regardless of possible social consequences, be prepared to have a non-combative consensus.

CONCLUSION

Emotional intelligence is an aspect of your general social media marketing strategy that you simply cannot do without. It gives you the opportunity to connect with the other person on a human / emotional level, and without that connection, you cannot go anywhere with the other person. Not only is it important that you develop emotional intelligence skills, but it is also very important that you surround yourself with people who have developed their sensitivity equally. If you manage to convince the other person that you are much better accepting what you offer, you have a lasting relationship.

Emotional intelligence is a key factor that significantly affects the probability of finding employment. Emotional Intelligence Quotient or EQ is the sociological term that refers to the group of personality traits, social thanks, communication, language, personal habits, kindness, attitudes and optimism that characterize a person. Its a measure of how well a person "fits" or excels in a particular social structure, the new potential job. According to most recruiters, headhunters and recruiters, there are two main aspects to recruitment / selection. that is, what an employer considers when making an employment decision. These are: (1) the technical or hard skills of a candidate and (2) the "fit" of a candidate, that is, chemistry, personality. This is probably not a surprise. However, what may surprise you is the impact that everyone has on the hiring decision. Technical skills are only 10-20% of the decision. In other words, "adjustment" represents 80-90% of the employment decision.

In view of this (in the context of the tense current labor market), the emotional intelligence of a respondent should be sharpened when entering the labor market, especially during job interviews.

However, the IQ is generally less important for success than the EQ. We all know academically bright and socially incompetent and unsuccessful people. What they lack is emotional intelligence. Given the importance of EQ for the recruitment process, measures must be taken to improve and improve them. You can improve the EQ simply by understanding the capabilities of the EQ. Here is a complete (but not complete) list of the capabilities or attributes that make up the EQ, in no particular order:

Ability to be a team player, to lead, participate, join and work effectively with a team.

Ability to lead, teach, train, inspire. Nonverbal communication skills; Corporal language. Strong ethnic work. Positive "winning" attitude. Ability to accept criticism, learn from them and be positive. Time management skills. Skills to solve problems. Self-confidence. Flexibility, adaptability. Auditory skills. Critical thinking Conflict resolution. Concentrated, driven. Action oriented. Motivation; Ability to motivate yourself and others. Works well under pressure. Negotiation skills. Radiate confidence. Creativity; Think in other directions. Multitasking and prioritization. Ability to read, listen and observe others. Ability to see the big picture. Political insight. Know yourself; Self-assessment capacity.

As your EQ improves, you need to discover how to control your emotions and behaviors. Then, you must learn to manage the behaviors necessary for a successful job interview and, ultimately, the business environment. To improve your EQ, a self-analysis and the following steps are suggested. Relieve stress quickly and reliably. Under a lot of stress, rational thinking and decisions are more difficult. Learn to deal with stress. Be tough Stay balanced, focused and under control. Connect with your emotions and feel comfortable with them. You need to understand your emotions and connect with them. You can't avoid your feelings. They have to be emotionally aware and handle them. Understand nonverbal communication and use it effectively. Nonverbal communication sends messages. They show that you are listening, that you are interested. You need to manage your nonverbal messages and read them from others. Use humor and play to face the challenges. Humor helps ease your burdens. Humor helps you overcome difficulties, overcome differences and promotes relaxation, energy and creativity. Resolve conflicts with self-confidence and self-confidence. Conflicts cannot be avoided. So learn to dissolve and manage it. Learn to spread and forgive.

Never stop helping others. An emotionally intelligent person has been described as a person who has found the most effective way to CONTROL and USE their emotions to achieve performance improvements and learning effects. From what has been said above, it can be rightly concluded that the ability to CONTROL and USE emotions to achieve the established objectives allows a person to be called emotionally intelligent.

By controlling your emotions, you allow the rational part of your mind to be involved in communication and decision making, which means that you think before reacting. If you allow your emotions to be under control, you react before thinking, and that can lead to conflict. Class discussions are a perfect example because you need to use a balance between logic and controlled emotions. This does not mean that you have to be free of emotions or expressions. However, you will discover that others are more willing to interact with you when they perceive it as a control over their responses and that they respond positively. This is a learned skill that can be developed and strengthened through practice over time. It can improve your performance, improve relationships and should be part of continuous personal self-development.

Why is self-knowledge important?

We need to be aware of what we feel to feel our behavioral responses to these feelings or emotions. Once this is done, we can take responsibility for our responses and control that behavior to reduce the impact on others and, ultimately, on ourselves. (This is the essence of cognitive behavioral therapy). We need to understand our own responses to pain, anger, even love and all our other emotions in order to adequately counteract other people and ourselves.

The truth is that the most successful people in work and life have the ability to manage themselves and their relationships with others. Social and emotional intelligence includes many skills, including stress management, resilience, productive conflict management, strong leverage, catalytic change, teamwork and collaboration, building trust and much more. Unfortunately, we see it more when it is not obvious: think of the boss who explodes when a deadline expires or the worker who does not trust his colleagues. Their behavioral response to what they feel affects us as much as our reactions to others. These people are limited by their lack of social and emotional skills.

Fortunately, adding these essential skills to your personal wellness and transformation strategy is never too late, and research shows that training and training are the fastest way to improve your social and emotional intelligence skills. There is always a reason not to change, there is always something or another person to blame for the situations in which we find ourselves, but if we look closely, we can find that they are our own problems that we encounter, then stress and frustration become huge! A good advice and guidance can provide and have a structured practical action plan to get out of the stress-related situation and arrive at a much better place.

Learning to manage pain, stress and anxiety, and learning the benefits of self-control, self-esteem and learning better social skills was a revelation and thought which was pretty good at all those things from the beginning! Getting a health check every now and then can be a good idea to identify problems before they get worse. Regular eye exams can be a great help in keeping your eyes healthy. However, how often do you take the time to check your personal emotional state and how does it affect your work and your private life? Emotional intelligence (EI) is the basis for the formation, development and mastery of social and personal emotional competencies, often referred to as "human abilities" that contribute to their success. The stronger your emotional competencies, the greater your success. The higher your level of emotional intelligence (EI), the more emotional skills you can learn and develop, and the better you can learn and develop those emotional skills, the greater your success. We all know the concept of a high IQ: the higher your IQ, the better you can learn, create, invent and solve what requires logical, technical or logical skills. In the same way, the more you develop your emotional intelligence, the better you can develop your emotional skills and more

Emotional intelligence is your innate or learned ability to acquire and apply the knowledge of your emotions and the emotions of others. With this information, you can make better decisions about what you say or do (or don't say or do) in a given situation. Emotional intelligence (EI) competences can be divided into two categories: intrapersonal (existing / occurring within the individual) and interpersonal (existing / occurring between individuals). The competences are logically based on each other. The former (emotional self-esteem, emotional self-regulation and emotional self-motivation) are intrapersonal and form the basis of interpersonal skills: empathy and relationship management. Emotional intelligence is a work from the inside out. Start with yourself: development of intrapersonal skills. The more experienced a manager or manager with emotional self-esteem, emotional self-regulation and emotional self-motivation, the easier it will be to capture the subtle social cues of others, be empathic and successfully manage relationships. Effective interpersonal skills depend largely on the development of effective intrapersonal skills.

Creating a solid foundation for emotional self-esteem increases the likelihood of developing strong competition in other competencies. Some measures that can be taken to improve the capacity for emotional self-awareness include ...Observe and name your emotions: when you can specify what you feel, you will receive information that will help you decide what to do or not to do or say in certain situations. Identify triggers of negative emotions: they can be people, events or situations that often trigger a strong negative emotional response. By recognizing triggers, the student knows when it may be useful to change or regulate their emotions (the second competence of EI, emotional self-regulation). Identify what is important in your life and what positive emotions it causes: these positive emotions are the emotions that the student wants to experience most frequently. The increasing frequency with which this type of emotions is experienced is related to a more positive energy. Research shows that thinking is clearer and better decisions are made when emotions are positive. It is often said that outstanding leaders have "good skills." But the person you know best is yourself. You start from the inside and work. The good news is that all these skills can be systematically learned, expanded and expanded. Emotional intelligence or EI is the ability to understand and control their own emotions and those of the people with whom they interact every day.

Pay attention to body language. Body language tells others how to feel in a situation and what message they convey. Body language can be a real advantage in a leadership role because you can see how someone really feels. This gives you the opportunity to respond appropriately. However, keep in mind that body language is not the most important aspect in determining a person's feelings. For example, when someone crosses their arms, it usually means that they are not open to discussions. Crossing the arms pushes an obstacle in front of the body to protect it. There are many people who intertwine their arms for reasons other than to exclude people. So be careful when reading body language. If you have a team member who is often asked to work late and reluctantly accepts it, you should try to solve the problem.

Social awareness and relationship management. They had problems with things like "tolerate frustration," "resist the desire to speak or act when the situation does not help," "improve mood in a room" and "manage conflicts effectively." Could it be surprising that informal team leaders who lack those skills have trouble effectively leading their teams?

By improving the EQ of all members of the self-directed teams, not just the informal leaders of the team, the teams act as more effective and more coherent units. The development of EQ capabilities throughout the organization requires the firm belief that EQ capabilities are critical to the success of each individual employee, since emotional intelligence in the workplace, like all important things in life you cannot buy or sell. Determine the problem. The development of equalization capabilities must include an accurate evaluation of the equalization of each individual. Create an action plan and take action. Emotional intelligence does not develop overnight, but it can be improved in weeks and months through a detailed action plan. The Emotional Intelligence Assessment not only identifies general points, but also specific problem areas within each equalization skill, providing a detailed and step-by-step process to improve these areas and improve equalization. E-learning activities and detailed strategies provide the necessary practice to develop new and productive habits. Reinforce the message. Last but not least, employees must be compatible with the system to improve their equalization capabilities. To stop emotional intelligence frustration requires that you are an emotionally intelligent manager, you work hard to build good relationships with your direct employees and your employer rewards you. They capture the moods of their employees and master the art of using the collective feelings of their team, both bitter and irrational, to achieve positive change and encourage constructive collaboration. When your team needs to meet, use your sophisticated emotional intelligence (EQ) to get results.

Do not go yet; One last thing to do

If you enjoyed this book or found it useful I'd be very grateful if you'd post a short review on it. Your support really does make a difference and I read all the reviews personally so I can get your feedback and make this book even better.

Thanks again for your support!

About the Author

Coleman Christy TANO is a highly regarded psychologist, author, and expert in the field of Cognitive Behavioral Therapy (CBT). With a wealth of clinical experience and a deep commitment to advancing mental health, TANO has become a prominent figure in the integration of research and practical applications within the realm of psychological well-being.

As an accomplished author, TANO brings a unique blend of academic insight and real-world understanding to the forefront. Known for translating complex psychological concepts into accessible and actionable strategies, TANO's work resonates with both mental health professionals and individuals seeking personal growth.

With a passion for empowering others to unlock their mental potential, TANO's contributions extend beyond the pages of "Mastering Cognitive Behavioral Therapy." Through workshops, lectures, and continued research, TANO actively contributes to the evolution of therapeutic practices, advocating for the widespread adoption of evidence-based approaches to enhance overall mental health.

Coleman Christy TANO's dedication to the field, combined with a compassionate approach to mental well-being, makes "Mastering Cognitive Behavioral Therapy" not just a guide but a testament to TANO's commitment to fostering positive change and transformation in the lives of individuals and the broader mental health community.